The first of a series of three volumes this book sets out the parameters for an uncomplicated spiritual philosophy that brings clarity and understanding to empower you to take control of your life and maintain health and wellbeing.

That Which Is

The Teachings of Herméas

Elizabeth Campbell

Martha E Randolph

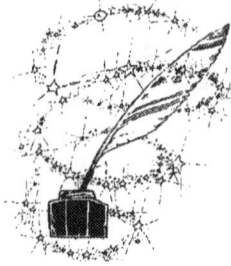

THAT WHICH IS

First Edition, 2007

Published by Cosmic Ink, 2007

ISBN: 978-0-6151-6352-9

Copyright © Elizabeth Campbell & Martha E Randolph, 2007

Typeset in 11pt Palatino Linotype by E Campbell Ltd

Design by Elizabeth Campbell

Contents

That Which Is

Before you, the reader, begin this book, there are some things that you must understand. Every concept expressed in this book, even those which are more scientific or technical in nature, are based on the understanding that life exists in order to learn, and that you have more than one chance to learn lessons.

That is to say, that life is continuous, and you have more than one life, it is the process of reincarnation – to create a form again.

There have been so many documented cases throughout history – especially in Tibet and India – that have shown that there are leaders (individuals such as the high Lamas) who will have a lifetime and then will be found again after their physical death, in the form of a young child. And that young child, usually being found at the age of three or four, will possess provable knowledge and wisdom of the former lifetime. There is only one purpose for such a precise event to occur, and that is essentially to act as documented proof of reincarnation.

By the same token, there are many documented "near death experiences", that clearly show that something other than the physical body of a human being, goes through some kind of process when the body ceases to function. That process is generally joy filled for those who have experienced it and come back – having gone through some profound change, usually involving them feeling a greater love and connection with the planet, and a greater sense of purpose.

Now, this ought be more than enough proof that there is more to your existence than just your physical body, and that your existence is continuous beyond the death of the body. But there are ingrained truths in every culture, which exist in order to allow the political and religious power structures to maintain control. The greatest control that any power structure has over humanity is the control of the life and death situation. Thus, the fear of dying is the ultimate fear. It is the fear most used and played upon to cause any number of actions to occur.

This is seen continually in international political affairs, such as the recent escalation of terrorist sponsored activities and the response by various world governments to those actions. It is the fear of being the next victim of any such act, the fear of being killed, the fear of dying, which has created the greatest reaction. No other act of violence or diminished state of existence so overwhelms us as this fear does.

Poverty, hunger, natural disaster, epidemic disease, do not seem to do it. If they were sufficient; pre-emptive actions would be taken to prevent or prepare for such events. Or governments would take equal action in response to such events as they do to acts of massive killing – but they don't. Actions are sometimes taken, but never to the same degree as when large numbers of dead bodies are seen and the threat of more death is present. **The fear of death is the most destructive force on your planet. It is the force that is most contrary to all evolution and all personal growth.**

In this book we have expressed many concepts. Some of them

are simple clarifications of truths that many of you will already have. Some of them may be completely innovative for you – a new viewpoint that you've never considered before, even about subjects with which you may be familiar.

In some cases there will be revelations, true revelations, but none of them will make any sense, or have any relevancy for you, if you truly believe that you have only one chance to exist, that you are born, you have a lifetime and you die, and then it is over, there is nothing. Neither will they be of much benefit to those who believe that you are born, you live a life, you die and then you either go to heaven, or to hell, or to some place in-between. At which point you remain a ghost of yourself, a spirit of your actual physical being forever, or until some religious event takes place.

If this is your unshakable truth and you are completely comfortable with it, then this book will not serve you in any way. If you still wish to read this book, be warned that if you do so, you may find a challenge to your truths, a challenge that is irrefutable if you look at the simple facts. Therefore you may choose not to read it, but wrap it nicely and give it to someone else.

* * *

Throughout this volume there shall be references to *The Story*[1]. It is a creation story. It is an analogy, a parable, imagery, if you will, to express to beings who are in physical form, the nature of *Creation* in its spiritual understanding. For there are in all things parallels between the creation of physical existence, energy, matter and all forces connected with it, and the spiritual essence of progression

---

1 *For those of you who wish to read The Story in its entirety we have included it in the back of the book. Please be aware The Story must be transmitted from one being to another at the appropriate frequency of energy, it is somewhat different when transmitted than the way it has been expressed here as the spoken word often doesn't translate to the written well but we have done our best to do it justice.*

that all beings undergo. This is the purpose for *The Story*.

In all religious texts there are variations of some creation story or another . Any being could read these stories and look for commonalities amongst them and find within that commonality a clarity, which is lacking in any one religious expression. However, this book is not for the purpose of religious expression, but for the simple purpose of understanding. If the images we are about to share with you in their briefness do not fulfil you; understand that they by themselves have no meaning, they are in essence symbolic. The purpose of *The Story* is to communicate an energy of remembrance to the individual experiencing *The Story*, so that he or she might remember the truth of their spiritual journey; the reason for which they exist today; the reason for which all existence came into being and the ultimate joy in the fulfilment of that purpose.

You have an Essential Spirit, which exists so that you may hold the sum of the knowledge of all of your lifetimes. You have a Soul Body, which you might call a ghost that will have the image of your physical body in any given lifetime. That soul embodiment will hold the experiences that you have in that lifetime and draw the lessons from them, take them, and incorporate them, into the Essential Spirit Body.

You will have many physical bodies. You will not, once you have emerged as a human physical body, return to lower miscellaneous forms. The human experiment, the life experience of an entity, does not cross over into the life experience of plants, minerals or animals.

You live a physical lifetime to have experiences, to which you react emotionally. You learn a lesson – about the nature of love and/or compassion. Your Essential Spirit is on a quest – a quest for the ultimate understanding of the nature of unconditional love with compassion.

On that quest, in order to achieve as great an understanding as possible, it is required of any entity to have experiences in a physical body. This may not be confined only to human form; it can be in another alien species form, but essentially it must be one that is compatible with your Essential Spirit.

For those beings who believe that they are aliens come again, an alien form may have once been used, but that is not who you essentially are, any more than you are only the physical being you are now. You are something more essential, something more continuous. If you cannot understand this or, if in some way, these thoughts offend; you are very much entitled to your truth. It is not wrong! For that is where your understanding currently exists, and you have a right to be in that place, but understand that if you have chosen to read on, there may be a reason. Perhaps it is time for you to consider other understandings.

May you read well – may you enjoy – may you grow in wisdom!

Herméas

Who Are You?

To answer questions regarding where this information comes from – who or what are you?

As already mentioned, your Essential Spirit creates a soul embodiment to hold emotion which then inhabits the physical body it is going to belong to in a given life time. That soul embodiment also carries with it aspects of what will become the personality suitable for that designated life time

Once a being is born into a life time, the essential personality reveals its own tendencies which come from its background. As a body grows and has experiences, it contributes to that personality, as it is part of the tool structure necessary to accomplish the lessons of any given lifetime. There is also an essential personality that belongs to the Essential Spirit, which always brings itself into aspects of any given lifetime, but which may or may not be a part of the given lifetimes personality structure.

At any one time, I am borrowing from several of a series of different lifetimes, multiple aspects of personality, to facilitate this communication.

In essence, I am a frequency of communication that comes directly from whatever you conceive of *The Source* as being. That communication is dampened somewhat to fit into the parameters of the listener's and the communicators understanding.

I am therefore as much of a being as any other being, existing at a higher frequency of vibration and therefore not in material form. I am using an illusion, very much like the outline of an animated figure that might be placed over a series of colour and sound vibrations, for the purpose of communication.

For me to say to your readers, things such as "I am God", "I am the Angel of God", "I am a spokesman for the Nine", "The Twelve", or whatever construct you are in alignment with, becomes in my opinion, a limitation and possibly confusing for the reader. That would make this book similar to other communications of this nature and that is not the intent of these communications.

The name that you refer to me by is Herméas[2], the more preferred pronunciation by myself, of the designation Hermes. It represents the Messenger of the Gods, that is, the individual personality vibration representing communication from *The Source*.

Obviously there is no individual God being, whose name is Hermes dressed in a white toga, with a little winged hat, sitting on top of a cloud on a mountain somewhere in Greece, who occasionally pops down to communicate with you. That is not at all that I am!

If the pronunciation of the name is confusing, then any being who is reading this material is more than welcome to refuse to acknowledge it. It has no more or no less significance than any of the other names that you understand my relationship to; Tehuti, for example, or any of the other wonderful ancient names corresponding to the Messenger of God (Hermes Trismegistus, Thoth, Quetzalcoatl, and Raphael). Those names are applied to define an essence of communication. A personality is used by the

2 *Pronounced Hur - may - ahs*

communication source to facilitate communication through an embodied agency. It is in the nature of human experience to define and name those things it must deal with, so that a focus can be maintained.

How do you recall an experience? How do you call into being an event? You understand it, focus it, visualise it, and name it, and then it has consistency. Every single time you wish to remember or repeat the experience, you have something specific to focus on. That is the reason for things such as names and personality vibrations.

Human beings must deal within a limited scope. That is the way it has always been. Thus, they have always tried to limit *That Which Is God* to an image that reflected themselves. The greater the understanding of the being, the less limited their vision of *That Which Is God*. This has happened throughout your history in every cultural reference.

So for those who have the widest scope of comprehension, who do not require limitations of focus, *I am that which exists at the vibratory frequency just slightly below the explosion of the universal bubble. The moment of creation comes into being - and I am.*

If you can comfortably conceive of that which comes into being immediately with the instant of creation, so be it. If that does not please you, or if you find that difficult to understand, then I may be considered a spirit representative of a very high vibrational form of information, as pure as is possible, connected to *That Which Is God,* or *The Source.* But not a God, not an individual being who is your Master, not that type of thing at all.

If you wish to excite the energies of those who read, you may say "there is none higher than myself and none lower. There is no source more pure – nor more stagnant". I am sorry that it cannot be made more simple for you, but if it was more simple it would be inaccurate and a condescension to your readers, and a compromise to the ethic of this writing.

There is nothing that occurs in the universe that I do not have some interest in. I have knowledge of all things, understanding of all things, and it brings me great joy. There is no existence, or form of existence with which I do not have direct communication and contact – regardless of how large or how small it may be. And there is no manifestation of being that I do not have some part of. So I am all-knowing, all-powerful and all-everything.

One might ask, isn't this God? - Indeed, and what is not God?

I do not wish to offend anyone, and as you well know there are those who acknowledge only one form of Divine expression, in the form of the teacher Jesus the Christ. In that case they will say "well are you Jesus?" Yes, I most certainly am, but that is not the only *"I am"* I am. It is not my intention to cause distress to those who have other beliefs by saying this, but avoiding such distress is not my main concern.

At this moment, I am here to add to the sum total of knowledge and information that is available in written and communicated form on this planet. It does not really matter what vibrational form the information comes through. What is important is the information itself, and what it means to you.

For *That Which Is* within you, and within every being, is in joy to hear this and will do with it what *It* can, within the limitation of the being *It* inhabits.

The *I Am* and I are one.

Microparticulars

The understanding of Microparticular Function is the key to healing and conscious control of your reality. Although this topic delves into the realm of Quantum Mechanics it is well worth the effort to understand. As we are all part of The One, we can, with practice, utilise microparticular function to participate consciously in our process. Microparticulars are referred to throughout this book so we felt it important to define the term for clearer understanding.

My first conscious experience with Microparticulars was during a trip to Monkey Mia[3]. I had gone there to take part in a chakra activation and had travelled by car for 11 ½ hours with a friend to get there. When we arrived all we wanted to do was say hello to the dolphins and go to bed. Much to our dismay (and excitement) we couldn't get to sleep, because there was a very active leyline[4] going right through the bedroom. Every time we closed our eyes there was a river of dancing light particles all flowing in the same direction; it was an amazing sight to see. We felt that this line linked the Monkey Mia chakra with those at Uluru (Ayers Rock) and Byron Bay as a conduit for communication and inter-dimensional travel. Interestingly

---

3   *An area north of Perth where dolphins have interacted with people for many years.*
4   *A channel of Earth energy*

enough it was not till the next morning, when we compared notes, that we discovered that we had both had identical, yet separate experiences.

I was later to discover, through our communications with Herméas that those dancing particles of light were the mechanism through which we can create our own reality – internally and externally. In his original description, Herméas hit us with "it is a spectromorgraphic field containing subnucleic microparticulars that vibrate at a rate of approximately 1,242,562 oscillations per nanosecond, very much like photons but smaller". As you can imagine that was as clear as mud, but eventually we decided to regard them as really tiny little guys who would do as you directed them as long as you were clear. After all, the concept of creating your own reality was hardly new to us; we simply didn't know the mechanics of the process.

This information became vitally important a few months later when a potentially life threatening health condition could no longer be ignored. By influencing the microparticulars of my body I was able to return an overstressed system to normal and repair a damaged valve in my heart. The technique is very simple, once you know the feeling of the frequency. – E

Microparticular is a phrase that we have created from Martha's vocabulary to describe something that has no explanation or definition within your current science.

Micro – meaning below the level of normal vision. It is so small that you would need to utilise magnification forces even greater than your current electron microscope and that device, being one that creates a still picture, cannot register the motion, which is essentially so rapid within the scope of its microscopic realm that it does not exist in the still picture.

Particular – meaning belonging to, or associated with a single person, group, thing, or category. We have utilised this word because we are not only talking about a particle.

It is a particle with a specific identity function, almost an intelligence, but again, that word does not suffice, because in your society, intelligence implies an individual will, and a microparticular does not have an individual will. It is a completely responsive unit, which can react without specific direction.

It reacts to intention and has its own understanding of what function it has to perform in response to that intention. So in a sense, it has intelligence – in the way you attribute intelligence to a hive mentality.

When dealing with the microparticulars within the structure of your body, the influence or intention is produced by your mind. The microparticulars are the masses, which have a function to perform. This is similar to the relationship between a Queen Bee and her hive. The hive will perform their function in response to the influence of the intention of the controlling force, regardless of the logic of that function or will perform default functions in the absence of any specific influence.

Microparticulars exist well below the level of the nucleotide[5], and really exist in such a balance of dimensions that you could go as microscopic as you wished and still have a hard time relating to them. In essence they are experienced as a sensation, an awareness, rather than something tangible.

Microparticulars function as a group, and each group knows the specific series of functions they need to perform. They can be

5   *A sub-unit of the double helix of DNA (deoxyribonucleic acid)*

swayed or directed by your intention, but when they get to where they are going, they perform their established function. You cannot change their function; you can only send in a different group of microparticulars to perform their own function.

Microparticulars have no awareness of what is good or bad, right or wrong; they simply perform their function. The performance and result of that function is dependent on the conscious or unconscious intention of the individual.

Thus, if you understood the world of the microparticular, you could perform genetic manipulation with the power of your mind – at least within your own embodiment – and you could cure all illnesses, regardless of their nature.

When working with microparticular structures it is more effective if you are clear about what it is you wish to have happen. Once the intention is clear, it is simply a process of going down inside your body to the frequency of vibration that is most conducive to transmitting your intention and allowing the microparticulars in their masses, to react in their own way as to the fulfilment of the intention.

In visualisation you might see them as a sort of opalescent light in motion. A river of flowing liquid light that has multiple colours moving in a specific direction, possibly accompanied by a particular sound.

When you wish to adjust the flow, you envisage a turning of the river to send it down another channelling conduit. This envisioning should not only change the direction and the tonality of the flow, but may also bring in other harmonic tonal attributes as well.

These are rather ephemeral descriptions, but because you cannot possibly envisage the actuality of a microparticular, you have to use allegory when working with them.

Even scientists will acknowledge that when they deal with the ultra-microscopic world, or the ultra-macroscopic world, they must estimate, envision and conceptualise. They cannot be as accurate as they would like to be, because, within the limitations of the current human mind's conceptual abilities, they cannot truly comprehend the totalities that exist over multiple billions of microns.

All things in the universe have at their roots a micro-particular structure, which coalesces itself to form the subnucleic particles that make up existence. These particles then come together in larger and larger groups and components, which begin to create structure. This is the case regardless of whether it is a mineral, gas, liquid or solid. It is the case, whether it is an interstellar piece of micro-matter, or an energy wave form or particle, or a quantum force such as dark matter or a planetary evolved structure like the human form. Microparticular structure is the one great constant. It may be envisioned as the bloodstream of *God.* That which flows continually throughout the universe and which, in its purest form, is completely directed by *That Which Is Divine.* And yet, you can influence it.

When you are contacting essences at that microscopic level you are contacting the most minute level of functioning of the essence of *God.* Just as when you go into the macroscopic level, (which is universal) you are contacting, you might say, the consciousness of *That Which Is God.* Thus, it brings you in a complete circle with two extreme frequencies, one extremely high, the other extremely low in vibrational frequency.

When we say microparticular we are speaking therefore, of the essential life force, which makes up all existence. Not the mind life force, but the structural life force – the essence of that which came into being in the instant of the big-bang – the first instant of all creation. It is an essence which from itself creates all forms. It is the structure of *God.* The embodiment of *God* if you will.

The Embodiments

In this section Herméas discusses the threefold structure of embodiment that is consistent throughout the book. Understanding of the structure is crucial to the understanding of the techniques and philosophies discussed here. The threefold structure does not discount previous concepts of seven bodies, plains of existence, or any other metaphysical teaching. It is a simplified construct, which we work with as a model for human existence. – E

The total understanding of the nature of the structure of a human being is part of the overall story of the nature of existence and creation. Covering how one came into being, why one came into being, what is one purpose, and eventual goal or direction. However, for the purpose of this work, the essential structure of a human being in the levels that we deal with, involves a threefold form.

The Essential Spirit

There is what we will call the Essential Spirit. The Essential Spirit is that which you are, and continues to exist throughout every lifetime. It is the part of you which assembles the information gathered through any lifetime and puts it together with other information.

It is the part of you that makes the decision as to the nature of life experience required in order to learn lessons in any given lifetime. It is the part of you that communicates with your guides and teachers, to accept influence and information regarding those choices.

The Essential Spirit has a visual presence, a personality, and an energy signature that is consistent. The image of that constantly growing, yet consistent entity, is reflected in your eye structure, and is reflected in all parts of the human body which prove to be unique and consistent.

Hand shape, fingerprint identity, certain characteristics of the ear, and, of course, the eyes, are consistent and individual to each person, regardless of who they are or where they come from. These reflections are the signature of your Essential Spirit, the form that you eventually return to when you vacate your body, and come from when you create a body.

The Soul Embodiment

The next level of embodiment is a lower frequency of vibration, slightly denser than the Essential Spirit. You may envision it as a garment which the Essential Spirit puts on in order to enter into and function within a physical embodiment.

We will call this embodiment the Soul Body. It is the non-physical image, the ghost or astral image of the physical body that is going to be inhabited, and is individual to a given lifetime.

The soul embodiment is created for the purpose of holding emotion, and acquiring information learned through emotional responses to actions and experiences. It is created by the Essential Spirit to define the physical embodiment it is going to enter.

Unless the goal of the soul embodiment is to experience the

emotional event of miscarriage or abortion, it is placed truly in the physical embodiment of a foetus when the commitment has been made for that child to be born.

I do not wish to get sidetracked on another issue, but it is important that there is recognition that you cannot prevent the birth of a being who is meant to be born.

Those who believe they are fighting for the life of a child, fail to understand that the Essential Spirit cannot be dissolved. Only physical matter returns to universal form, and the soul embodiment is temporarily released and then placed into another embodiment when its time comes.

There is nothing wrong with abortion as a process. It is a relationship and experience that the Essential Spirits of mother and child have to experience at some time in their existence in order to understand the nature of life, its sacredness, and one's attitude towards life and death[6].

Now, to get back to the subject at hand. Once the irrevocable choice is made to be born in a physical form, the soul embodiment enters, encloses, and begins to define the shape of the physical body that is going to be born upon the planet. This may take place while the child is in the womb of the mother, therefore establishing unique levels of communication between mother and child; as many women have experienced. Usually the choice to experience the birth process is made after a length of time, while the body is forming.

The Physical Embodiment

The Essential Spirit searches for an appropriate physical form that will be born into a specific parental environment. It selects from the

---

6 *Usually once it is experienced it is not required to be repeated.*

wide range of children being initiated, the one most appropriate to its own lessons, as well as for the lesson plans of the adults who have participated in the creating of the child. Once the selection has been made the soul embodiment enters that physical form and subtle changes take place to match the physical form to the soul embodiment.

The initial act of producing a child is part of the life experience of the parents. The nature of what that child will be, and how it will go through its life experiences, is made by its Essential Spirit.

From the moment the physical body is born into consciousness upon the planet, it begins to register physical experiences. Those experiences are reacted to by its soul embodiment, which creates wisdom information that is recorded within the soul embodiment to be observed (but not interfered with) by the Essential Spirit.

All physical experiences, regardless of whether they are joy filled, or traumatic, teach the being. When the Soul Body has an emotional reaction, knowledge is gained and kept in storage. But that knowledge is not assimilated in totality by the Essential Spirit until the death of the physical body.

One of the most important acts that you can experience in a body is getting in touch with your Higher Self. It is more objective than your soul, and understands the plan. So the more you try to get in touch with your higher vibration (which has created your life experiences) the smoother the transition becomes.

The lessons must still be learned, but the learning process can be made more rapid and direct; thereby eliminating unnecessary hardship. At all times free will is retained, but it is responding to the plan of your higher self. So when a person feels their life is out of control, it is only the physical embodiment that is not in control – it is their higher self that is in control. Their Essential Spirit is in command, because the control was established when they were born. Thus, contact with your higher self enables you to understand more quickly the reasons for things happening, so they will not affect you in such an emotional way.

The physical body is designed to have experiences. The soul embodiment reacts emotionally to those experiences, and from those emotions, gains wisdom. The wisdom is eventually assimilated by the higher self, or Essential Spirit. The soul embodiment is not designed to have a permanent existence. It is only the astral or non-material image of the physical body it inhabits in any given lifetime.

The Essential Spirit holds the assembled wisdom of all your lifetimes and is consistent in its image, appearance and personality, which is not always the same as the physical body it is inhabiting in a given lifetime.

You may recognise the Essential Spirit of another being by eye contact, hand shape, fingerprint signature, or structure of the internal ear. These features are individual to each being and are defined by the Essential Spirit. Thus you will always recognise the past life acquaintances with whom you had particular connection, through eye contact or the touching of hands.

This recognition is one of the reasons why some cultures encourage physical contact, and others require that you do not contact. There are cultures that prefer not to touch, and whose eyes will drop when you look at them. This comes from a wish not to be recognised, and not to recognise. There are other cultures that require a great deal of physical contact – the touching of hands, the looking into eyes, the embracing of the being. The more contact you have, the more recognition you may experience.

Cellular Memory

Let me explain how this ties in with other truths, such as cellular memory. The microparticular structures that come together to create your physical body exist as a unit responsive individually to your Essential Spirit. Thus, whenever your Essential Spirit is going to create a physical body, it uses the same microparticular structures, which are also parts of itself.

The microparticular structures are in constant contact with the Essential Spirit and respond to its requirements during an individual lifetime. For example, if it is necessary that a being is to be permanently crippled, the microparticular structure (whose inclination would be to form a perfect physical unit) will respond to the direction of the Essential Spirit and create the desired adjustment.

The microparticular structures carry with them a complete memory of the wisdom of all the Being's lifetimes. Therefore, everything experienced by the Essential Spirit of a being is recorded in the microparticulars which created the matter.

If an experience has not been completely absorbed as wisdom by the Essential Spirit, the microparticulars that were part of that experience will retain the awareness of that experience instead of adding it to the accumulated wisdom. They are therefore reborn into the physical body with the experience still having some affect. Thus, a person may have a chronic pain which is not related to their current lifetime. This is cellular memory – an experience which is not completely absorbed and filed by the microparticulars which make up the cells of the affected part of the physical body.

When someone treats that area of the physical body and causes the memory of that lifetime to be addressed, the microparticulars, which still remember that experience, carry the message that you are having that experience, so that the conscious mind will direct its attention to it. The conscious mind then takes the experience, reforms it and absorbs the knowledge required from it so that those microparticulars can go back to living in the way they were supposed to function in the current life-plane.

The Essential Spirit, soul embodiment and physical embodiment are the three embodiments that human beings deal with most frequently, including those beings who are dealing with levels of spiritual understanding.

Your higher self is different from your guides or guardian angels, or the influences of councils. For the purpose of this publication we will not go into the details of those separations. When spiritual teachings discuss seven, nine or twelve embodiments, they are dealing with higher and higher frequencies of vibrational awareness of existence. If we are going to deal with those we are going to get into complications which will not be appropriate until we get to the end of this particular volume. Therefore, at this point we will define only the threefold human as it exists in its understanding of existence and dimensional reality.

Genetics and the Embodiments

The genetics of the physical form are defined by the microparticular structure. The Essential Spirit chooses to place its soul embodiment into the genetic structure which will be most efficient for its needs.

This is extremely complicated to explain. Because the more you pursue this thought, the more you will bring yourself back to the way in which whole universes, and multiple universes, work in agreement with all of *Itself.*

There is a seeming contradiction in the way I have explained that a soul embodiment is placed in a physical structure. One who is astute will question how, if the microparticulars are supposed to be specific to soul embodiment, is it possible to place a soul embodiment in a physical structure that is already been engendered by two beings?

We then get into the complications of how all things work together to create that which must be. There must always be the understanding of *That Which Is in control.*

The Divine Plan which effects and influences the choices made by an Essential Spirit is outside the conscious awareness of the Essential Spirit. The Essential Spirit is not all consciousness and awareness above certain frequencies. Thus, you might say there is an overall awareness that knows before the Essential Spirit knows, what lesson it will choose, what embodiment it needs, and which parents are going to be required.

Therefore the microparticular structure is engendered appropriately from this greater awareness.

I do not wish to explore that further at this time, as it creates too many paradoxes for the mind to deal with, and we are already going to indulge our readers with a number of interesting paradoxes, which will hopefully set them to thinking a great deal.

The Nature of Learning Lessons

The way in which body and cellular structure absorb information. The reason why certain information does not seem to be absorbed and sometimes lingers. Why lessons must be repeated and the real process behind that. The nature of this wonderful review and why it is even necessary.

The process of lessons is the education of your Essential Spirit; moving back to a place where its awareness of itself is expanded to the degree that it remembers its own birth. Because that birth is a moment of such extraordinarily high energy and since the essence of that energy is all encompassing, (the understanding of love, compassion and caring) there is simply no limit to the number of experiences that can enhance that understanding.

Repeated Lessons

Any learning process should allow a certain amount of lee-way. Physical and soul embodiment structures must have achieved the understanding of the lesson learned, in order to have a lesson completed. A percentage of the physical structure of the body, and its microparticular intelligences, must accept an understanding of a lesson before it becomes totally owned by the soul embodiment and is passed on to the Essential Spirit.

Repeated lessons come about because the correct amount of

acceptance was not achieved in a given lesson. For example, you have an experience with someone who does not treat you well. It is not enough if only 50 per cent of your physical structure has accepted that such treatment is no longer desirable.

Every repeated experience teaches some physical part of your body this truth, again. The trouble is the physical part that learned the lesson doesn't hold on to the information while the other 50 per cent catches up. If the lesson is not learned, there tends to be forgetfulness, so that you actually lose a very significant amount of what you have learned. You start again and build up to a higher amount. You don't lose it all. Otherwise you could not learn as quickly as you do. With repeated experiences the lesson takes less time, and eventually the correct percentage of the physical body communicates the acceptance of the lesson to the soul embodiment so that repetitions are no longer needed.

When a very difficult lesson has been learned, there are patterns of cellular memory in your microparticulars, which are automatically conditioned to think they are going to forget again. Thus, a review occurs; it is a reminder for transmission. The physical body has received the percentage necessary to accept a lesson, and now there must be a transmission into the Soul Body, which will accept it completely into the area of itself that houses information.

Sometimes when a lesson has been extremely difficult, the physical body holds onto the information and does not transmit. Although the learning has been achieved, there is still a certain amount of doubt, almost an expectation of forgetting again. This is when a review lesson is required; calling on the body to consciously acknowledge that learning has taken place, and which lesson was learned.

In that moment of conscious awareness, the body acknowledges that this was the lesson; this is what was learned, and its relationship to it. The lesson passes through in that moment without having to be repeated – it is just a review, or a signal. The information passes from the physical body, through to the soul embodiment into that area wherein the information is retained for further record. It becomes an essential part of you.

From that point on, the information becomes so ingrained in you, that your responses will never be the same again, and you won't even know why. You will never have to deal with the same situation again. The difficulty for some people, is that even though they have learned their lessons, they still expect something to happen which will require them to re-enact the scenario.

The review, once it takes place, eliminates that need, and the process from that time forward, is a complete acceptance of a way of being. Thus, the person begins to change, to the point where individuals who know them would say that they seem to be different. Usually the reaction seems to be that they are more mature, quieter, more internal, and have grown in some way.

Within the learning process, the body learns by the use of the senses. These include not only the five that your body is most familiar with, but also the other senses that you are beginning to consider now as your natural birthright. These senses exist as part of your physical body and auric field – which is also part of your physical body[7].

---

7 *The aura is not the soul. People mistake this, so let us be clear. The aura is a radiant energy emanating from the physical body. It reflects the well-being of the physical body which is affected by the mind. The mind of course, has a strong relationship with the soul and the Essential Spirit. Therefore, there is a confusion that the auric body is the one that goes travelling. Not so; the soul embodiment goes travelling, the auric field may or may not choose to go with the Soul Body. Does a sleeping body have aura? Of course. Yet a sleeping being is most likely to allow itself to go travelling.*

Sometimes, if one particular area of the body has been focused upon for a lesson, that area of the body will isolate the experience in an automatic need to protect the rest of the body from the unpleasantness of the experience. This is usually brought to light in the case of some kind of flashback, or physical action response. It is a microparticular autonomic function to surround and protect when an area has been traumatised, so that the whole being does not react. For example, let us say that you have been stabbed. Instead of your whole body and soul reacting as if it has been cut, the trauma is isolated to one area. There is pain, and related emotional responses, but they are isolated to the area of injury. Consequently that area can become the repository for the experience. It may not be absorbed as a total experience into the Soul Body, because learning requires a certain amount of conscious awareness.

Thus, where there has been a traumatic experience in a past life, lessons that have not been absorbed can be isolated to one area of the body, because the conscious awareness of the being was so shocked by the experience. There was no absorption of understanding, as the being was in protection mode. It does not halt the learning process, because every human being who has ever suppressed a lesson will undergo an experience where the memory is eventually called up for some reason or another, and is then absorbed.

The microparticulars that make up your physical form are the same ones that have always made up your physical form, regardless of what lifetime you are in. They are simply re-arranged in another way. Thus, the microparticulars (sub-nucleic – below the level of the atom) are the energies that create the atoms, which link up to

---

The aura is the electromagnetic energy emanating from the physical body and reflects the mental health just as the physical body reflects the mental health. It reflects the soul health and wisdom as the body reflects the soul health and wisdom. – H

create the molecules, which link up to create the body.

Memories travel with you, because it is the same set of microparticulars making up your form. The eyes are a reflection of your Essential Spirit in every lifetime. They change only in the way the Essential Spirit grows and changes, but always with the recognition codes within them. They reflect not only the physical being but they also have a recognition code within them, which can create a communication from Essential Spirit to Essential Spirit. This is the basis of the phrase, "The eyes are the window to the soul."

You always recognise a being and the past lives you have lived with them, through the eyes, because of the consistency in their recognition code, even though features may change. Although, they do adjust to developments in the Essential Spirit and the requirements of the physical body they are in. As you know, the health of the physical body are reflected in the pattern of the iris, but that is separate from the recognition code and from those essential elements that travel through every lifetime.

The microparticulars of your body are essentially your own set, and they reform and adjust themselves from infancy. When you are born on the planet they can carry any unlearned lessons from previous lives with them. As you grow up, it is possible for chronic problems to develop that are related to a lesson that was isolated and not absorbed. Since you are not directly in the experience, it is possible to use regression or a hands-on-healing technique to connect with the memory, so it can be adjusted and the lesson absorbed.

There are cases where enough of the physical body has absorbed a lesson, but it has not penetrated through the Soul Body into the Essential Spirit, because the trauma was isolated. When the Being comes back into a body, the trigger point remains in the area that must be addressed, in order to cause the transition of the information through to the soul embodiment.

Conscious participation and awareness enhance the process, and the more fully one lives any given experience, the more rapidity it will be absorbed. The reason you are developing into a more conscious being, is to speed up the process. That is the point of increased consciousness.

The Choice to Complete[8]

There is a very real perception that lifetimes go on *ad infinitum*, because there is so much to be learned, there is always at any moment, another nuance of understanding to be acquired in the remembering of the essence of *That Which Is God,* the loving thought and the infinite compassion. That is why it is possible for a being never to stop its cycle, and continuous exploration is possible.

In order for completion to occur there has to be a choice; the specific will or focus, which says "I no longer want to continue in endless cycles, I wish to achieve completion, understanding, and totality". This must be a conscious thought; a leap of understanding is then required. You go from a learning process, which has you acquiring infor-mation a step at a time, to an explosion of understanding, which does not require the filling in of every little detail.

Consider this to be like painting by numbers. Only in this case, you have numbers for every infinitesimal space in the procedure. In order to complete the picture you fill in each number – with each lifetime providing you with the experiences to fill in some of these numbers. The misunderstanding is that the process is such that you must fill in each number before you complete the picture. If it

8 *This refers to the choosing of completion as outlined in The Story*

was a mechanical process, this would be true – but it is not.

Once a certain amount of the picture has been completed, it is possible to commit a leap of understanding. Some of the picture does not exist but there is no requirement to fill in each nuance. Each being has a different point at which they will reach that trigger; beyond which they can make an intuitive leap into understanding, at any time – it is similar to the Hundredth Monkey Effect[9]. The prime ingredient for making that intuitive leap is the wish to do so, and the recognition that such a leap is what is required.

The most important thing in spiritual evolvement is to want this completion. Wanting it is primary, because you cannot achieve the intuitive leap without the wanting. But wanting does not necessarily mean it has to happen in any specific given lifetime, nor is there one particular way in which it needs to take place. What is required to make that leap is unique to each being.

Once the decision has been made, there are still some elements of the picture that must be filled in. Because once the goal has been specified a process of acceleration takes place. The educational process is sped up and narrowed down at the same time, and the degree of awareness has been reached where one perceives that an intuitive leap is possible.

Then the choice is made as to which elements (or numbers) must be filled in, to allow the intuitive leap to take place. For the choice to be made, there must be the will to do it, the recognition of the possibility of achieving it, and the desire to do it.

Now comes the change of plan. This is a unique experience in the life of any being, because this event by itself can change their entire learning programme. The complete karmic structure of the

9   Referring to research that shows learned behaviour can be transmitted through collective consciousness.

being's lifetime, (whatever they came in to learn) may be altered. This moment, when it occurs, is their own choice, and it can be offered at any given time.

There is no specification in the plan initiated by the Essential Spirit, which indicates they will be offered this choice in this lifetime. The plan is simply to acquire information, so that when the choice is offered, there is enough stored to allow the consideration of acceptance. It is determined by those who are in a body[10], and consciously aware that their job is to recognise the state of rightness in the being, and offer this chance of completion. This choice is one of the most real moments of free will an individual will ever encounter.

Free will is a questionable concept. There is of course, freedom of choice in many areas, but usually that freedom has already been exercised in another state of being. The exercise of free will, on the spiritual plane, can result in some aspects of physical life no longer being completely free. There are a series of choices that may be made within any lifetime, or structure of learning. However, the lesson plan has been made and certain things must happen as planned.

Because it is such a personal and dramatic choice this moment of choosing completion is very free, but it is a choice which once made cannot be unmade. There is a difference between saying "I want," and really making the choice. It is not just a matter of saying the words.

The three elements of creation – the thought, then the word, and then the action

When you have a thought, you speak the word, then the word

---

10 *Those teachers who have achieved the degree of understanding very close to what you would call mastery, who have already made their choice and have elected to maintain a presence on the planet to assist others.*

must be put into action. "Into action" means your considered effort, your constant thought/word/action processes being repeated as you move in that continual direction towards *Totality* – total knowledge, amalgamation, and unity. This, of course, requires some vision of what it is you want.

It is acknowledged that you will only be able to come up with symbology for this concept. It is impossible for you to truly envision that *Totality*, because in the moment you envision it, you become it. There is some understanding of that sublime moment of instantaneous creation that echoes in the memory of every being and some concept of it must exist in the being for them to make this choice.

It is not necessary for people to choose completion. Therefore it would be correct for people to say that in their understanding, there is a never-ending series of lifetimes, that there is no ending. Although there is no ending as we conceive of ending, there is a difference between the path of one who has chosen to remember their *Totality*, and the path of one following what was chosen – to constantly explore the concept of *Totality*.

It is like being a perpetual student, as a student in the university of life-never-ending there is always something new to learn; and then there are those who chose to graduate. Graduation can be a very frightening thing, because much of what you have come to rely on to give you focus and structure is no longer there.

Thus it is the same for the Essential Spirit. An Essential Spirit has its own personality and essence, and there is such a thing as an Essential Spirit that has less courage or will than another Essential Spirit. This is not a judgement. It doesn't make them good or bad, but does determine why there isn't a never-ending supply of evolving masters reaching enlightenment, at any given moment. Again these are very inadequate terms, but I am trying to use the language that you are accustomed to.

Accelerated Consciousness

One of the aspects of this New Age was to consciously take command of this learning process and willingly transfer experiences from the physical body directly into the Soul Body. It is the purpose of consciousness to go into any experience with the awareness of the learning process in order to get a high percentage of cellular structure to accept the lesson.

Being in communication with non-material spirits is not necessarily consciousness. The word "consciousness" refers to deliberately being aware and awake, which therefore can be applied to any number of things. But in your physical body, consciousness refers to the active learning process, and your participation in that process. You might see it as attacking life, rather than passively allowing life to pass by. When a being consciously chooses to accept the goal of completion, the process of accelerated consciousness begins, and becomes vitally necessary.

Thus, you might say that for those beings who have made this choice, increased consciousness is automatic, they must acquire it. Those who have not made this choice can go on quite comfortably semi-conscious. Once a being has accepted that death is not an ending, that life is a series of continual lifetimes and lesson processes, they may choose to relax in that belief and allow it to play through.

Although this is acceptable, it is not higher consciousness. This is new information. Yes! It is a higher consciousness than the one prior to it, but it is not anywhere near the concept that you might refer to as enlightenment. It is no more enlightened consciousness than a heat flash up the spine is the rising of the kundalini[11].

I do not mean to discourage those who do not wish to make this choice. It is not an unconscious thought for those who are offered a choice to say, "Not now, thank you very much; I would rather continue the process I am in." That is a choice made, and they then have the option to pursue their learning process more or less actively. But for those beings, who have never considered the thought, let us say they are living life a little bit less productively than they might be, in terms of lesson learning.

So if nothing else, let us offer this choice somewhere in this publication. It is possible, and indeed the purpose of humanity in coming here, is to achieve a point of completion. However, it is not absolutely required that every being make this choice, and certainly not at any given time. The choice exists. Whether or not you make it, or simply are aware of it will determine how you live your life and utilise spiritual tools.

Those who know there is a choice in the first place are separated from those who do not. Then within that, to choose completion, or not, also creates separation. But the choice to avail oneself of the choice or not, gives you the fine line between those who dabble and those who change their lives. For even the conscious choice not to complete is a step towards a higher consciousness and greater awareness, because you have accepted that you are in a learning process and that you want to be learning.

---

[11] *There is very casual commentary on the raising of kundalini, and it is a most horrific misnomer. It is a misuse of a word that represents an energy which by rights, for anyone who does raise it, would burn them to a cinder if they were not already close to Christ C   onsciousness. The kundalini, in its true highly pure and energised form, is essentially a power beyond the control of even very enlightened beings.*

Those who believe that they are doing a kundalini type of yoga or raising their energy are really raising, shall we say, just a flicker of a related energy. If they wish to call it kundalini, that is fine, they may call it anything they wish, but it is not an accurate term. – H

Therefore, it is logical that those who wish to process through to completion will be even more aggressive in their approach to learning lessons. They indeed, must become more conscious, because without realising it they want to reach that point where enough of the picture has been completed to allow for instantaneous inspiration. The leap of faith. The leap of intuition.

For conscious beings, I encourage you to make all of these events, moments wherein you think about the relationship that you have to your deepening understanding of the nature of God, and your relationship to *That Which Is God*. This is the conscious step, and if it sounds a bit like the religious fanaticism of those in monasteries; yes, it is very much like it. The difference is you are not in a monastery. You function on a daily basis in interaction with many beings. It is not only about you as a being, and how you will deal with other beings, but also the deeper lesson.

You must go with the trust! The deeper trust. The trust that goes so far that you do not question, the trust of a Master – someone who has the complete picture, who knows without knowing how, that all that is required will occur. It happens instantaneously at the moment that the need exists, and there is no need to know how. There is an attunement so divine that it is complete in its totality of trust. Because you know that **you** are *That Which Is God*.

That Which Is God is the original creative force, and all things are of it. So what God needs of God is surely manifested by God, in any given instant. If you live that truth in your ordinary everyday life, you become a living example for many others, and inner simplicity becomes more and more simple.

When enough of the microparticular cellular structure of your body has absorbed the recognition that they are *That Which Is God*, and all their requirements are instantly met, (as God manifesting in form) you become a Master. The lesson has been learned. It penetrates through your Soul Body, and is transmitted to your Essential Spirit. In that moment there begins to come into being, a living unity in those three vibrational forms of your existence – Essential Spirit, soul embodiment and physical body.

They begin to amalgamate and join. The physical body begins to accelerate its vibration so that it begins to mould itself more into the soul embodiment, which is a much lighter essence, an emotional essence. Then the Soul naturally begins to lessen its attachment to emotional lessons and becomes more in alignment with the Essential Spirit. Thus the physical body begins to change, to resemble the Essential Spirit more. You will actually see such a change take place, and others will see it as well.

This will happen whether you will it or not, as it is part of the process. There is of course resistance, but it is the resistance that comes from the fear that success will not be achieved, and the judgement of not achieving that success. Once a goal like this has been chosen there is always an aspect of the being that fears that they are unworthy to achieve, and the doubts and fears set up a pattern of pulling back from the commitment.

This fear exists to give comfort, so that if a certain degree of evolution has not been achieved one can simply say "Well I was just not good enough." That is simply not so. You cannot be offered the choice until you are ready to make it. If you have achieved a level of perception great enough to choose completion, then you are not only good enough, but also you are considerably better than you know. It is the most powerful of choices.

What you are thinking of doing, requires the deepest understanding of the nature of existence, and the surrender (almost in totality) of the very essence of ego into the love of being – the love of existence in all of its multiple forms.

This is indeed a great understanding.

Karma

Karma as it is conventionally used -- implying inevitable retribution of sorts.

"For every action there is an equal and opposite reaction. In the sense of spiritual understanding, the implication is that these equal and opposite reactions may take place over any number of lifetimes. This is Karma and this is essentially true.

This is also the difference between Karma and the term "cause and effect" as it is most often used today. Karma usually refers to action/reaction influences over multiple life times, while "cause and effect" usually refers to that principle within a specific life time.

In a balanced Spiritual Universe, any action/cause, will produce a balanced response/effect. However as there is no such thing as time in the Spiritual Universe, there is no limitation as to when this response/effect may take place. The concept of Karma, as it is commonly used today, does not necessarily acknowledge the influence on Karmic activity by the power of choice initiated by the individual, in conjunction with the guiding energies involved with that individual[12].

---

12 *The teachers, who assist the individual when outside the body, to make choices about the lessons to be learned and the methods through which that individual lifetime will acquire those lessons.*

Simply put, Karma is the most effective way of acquiring information. It is *almost* inevitable that in order to truly understand any given experience, one will have to experience the event from all possible viewpoints. When a truly significant lesson must be learned, it is very important to experience it from all sides. If you have performed a series of actions in any given lifetime, which have caused disruption, or caused certain reactions within that lifetime, then it is most probable that you will be placed into the other experiences generated by those actions.

Through this process your higher self will absorb the total impact of the wisdom in that experience. Or to put it even more simply – **in order to get it, you have to check it out from all sides**, living it and experiencing it.

Once outside the body, the essential truth of every being is the constant pursuit of wisdom and the understanding of the nature of existence. This is the essential goal of all beings, regardless of what they think is their truth in any given lifetime.

Once freed from the limitations of the physical incarnation, there is an awareness of the consistent push towards a higher goal, a deeper understanding. And since you are then separated from the pain and agonies of the physical body, you are in the position to understand that they are all part of the process. From this perspective, there is no hesitation in creating a lifetime where you receive the opposite experience, even if it is very unpleasant. Therefore, you use the tool referred to as Karma; because it is the best tool available. However it is not always   absolutely required; there is flexibility within all processes and tools in the Spiritual Universe.

The more conscious a being becomes while in a body, the more frequently and quickly they will cleanse and complete a learning experience. This can often occur within the current lifetime or even better within the hour. You do not require the re-experiencing of the event (or a similar event) from all sides if you have analysed it from all angles. This would be accomplished by placing your awareness in the other perspectives of a situation and therefore experiencing it in totality. In this way you can consciously gain both the immediate knowledge and the broader universal wisdom the experience was designed to provide.

Essentially this is the difference between a <u>conscious</u> being, and a <u>semi-conscious</u> being.

I do not use the term unconscious, although in many cases the difference between the unconscious and the semi-conscious is minute. But in your language unconscious means the same thing as sleep or a state of physical non-functioning and therefore, I use the term semi-conscious. It is unfortunately, the state of awareness that 99% of humanity function in most of the time; including those beings who are making an effort to be more aware. Their consciousness comes into play when they make an effort to put it into play, but in everyday situations they tend to coast at a level of semi-consciousness to one degree or another.

What is the difference between a conscious being and a semi-conscious being?

The conscious awareness of what you are doing, and taking action to do it, is the behaviour of a conscious being. You do not stop learning. You do not stop having experiences. You do not awaken one morning in perfection. You must continue to grow; but the difference is that you grow consciously. You know that this is your process, you see it, you feel it, you don't stop it, you allow it to go on, but you proceed with awareness. You are in it, and watching it at the same time. So you use it more effectively. That is essentially Karma.

When that outside action occurs, a conscious being may re-examine the situation and try to place him/herself (using imagination and envisioning capabilities) in the position of the person who was on the receiving end of the initial actions, to discover how it feels to experience the situation from their point of view. It is the act of a conscious being to recognise for whatever reason, that a personal truth may not be absolute.

It is a conscious act, for an individual who has been in conflict with another individual all of their lives, to be brought to the point where they take a moment to say, "I wonder if I can look at myself through their eyes. How do I see my own actions? How do they receive them?"

The very simple act of attempting to understand the way in which another views you, or any series of actions greatly assists communication between individuals, and the development of world (and indeed universal) peace and co-operation. The ability to put this into practice is very much connected to one's security in one's self. When you are self-confident you are free to examine another's choices which may differ from yours. Because when you feel content with your own choices you do not feel the need to defend them. If you are insecure, or feel threatened, you have no room to question, because those questions are your own doubts and fears, being reflected to you by the other person.

The inevitability of Karma

Karma is the best tool for acquiring wisdom from a physical learning experience. It is therefore used so consistently that it has taken on the appearance of being practically inevitable. Given the situations in which it is used, it would seem to be that way. I only acknowledge to you that truly conscious beings, who are aware of the use of the common experience, can cleanse an experience completely, before karmic education manifests, Because once they are aware it is a leaning experience, like an eager student, they can do the extra work and avoid the more intensive and often unpleasant repercussions of the Karmic system of learning lessons.

Karma usually gains its power over the actions of other human beings, because it is viewed as a threat, and that can be brought out of proportion in the debate, making it more important than it is.

A lifetime exists for you to continue your search. The search is the learning of wisdom derived from experiencing the deeper understanding of the nature of God, all that is, and compassion. This exquisitely constructed tool of learning exists for this purpose. You cannot escape it, because the truth is, once you understand it, you don't want to. But you can eliminate the need for it, by consciously taking the action that Karma supplies for you unconsciously. What can be simpler than that?

By being aware of the process and taking steps to speed it up and make it more effective, you are participating with *The Divine* in the process of your constantly increasing evolvement, and awareness of *That Which Is*. It is the balance between accepting responsibility, and taking action to participate with the *Universal Force*, and relinquishing control (not trying to manipulate it), while still allowing the force to guide you.

The aim is that wonderful delicate point where you do not try to make the lesson, but you let it present itself. Then as it becomes very clear, you consciously go forward into it. The balance is not to rush in too quickly, so that you change or manipulate the lesson to what you think it should be, but relinquish control to the degree that you allow the lesson to emerge, very clearly. You recognise that it is a lesson; you understand the nature of the lesson, and your part in it, and then take action immediately to resolve and relinquish it. Then you relinquish control and allow the next lesson to come forth. This is the intricate balance, which proves to be so difficult for many beings of power; as they find that balance between accepting responsibility and taking control of their lives.

There are many people who have very hard lives. Once out of the body, the harshness is clearly perceived as no more nor less than the necessary experiences for that beings spiritual evolvement. All beings will undergo every single trauma the body may experience before they are done with physical incarnation. You cannot equivocate by allowing your growing compassion, to say to you "But I don't like this part of *The Story*, it does not seem to be caring." Well, in that sense it's not. It is allowing. You must learn the balance between unconditional love, which is impersonal; and compassion, which cares and empathizes, yet will not interfere with the experience.

What will be learned in any given lifetime is your own choice! But it is a choice made by you from the objective position of your essential spirit. It is obviously not the conscious choice of any being when they are in the body, to experience trauma. You feel put upon, you are hurting, and you do not know why. You wonder what you have done to deserve this.

No child is born onto the planet with the awareness of the trials to come. You are born perfect, very pure, very honest, believing in your own right to be loved. Every child is born that way, so that they may begin to experience the conflicts they need to understand the nature of expressing and receiving expressions of love. In order to manifest this lesson, you forget what you already know. That is the process.

I do not know any sane person who would choose to suffer if they were in conscious awareness of all of what was required. If you take someone, no matter whether they are a child or an adult, and say to them "By the way, the rest of your life reads this way, and you will be raped and strangled and killed. Would you like to continue?" Most intelligent beings would say "No thank you very much, I would rather not continue in this way." Even if you inform them that it is the only way to learn these lessons, and that they will feel better about it when they are out of the body, they are not going to accept it.

They are in the body! They will not want to do this. Why would anyone want to do so?

This has been the essential manipulation used by many of your organised religions in order to maintain their power. They preach that even though you are poor and suffering in this life, you will receive your reward when you are dead. Therefore you should maintain your position and be at peace.

Karma then becomes a truth which is bent, twisted and manipulated, to be used as a tool for oppression. Instead of the truth, which is – you may be suffering now, but there is a purpose for it, and you will learn something in the process, and when you are finished with this life, you will be in joy to have learned what you have. The pain will not go with you.

This does not mean that a person does not have the right to strive for something else. When they are in a lifetime, it is their time, their reality. Within their understanding of the growth of themselves, and their growth of compassion, they have a right, and indeed an obligation to do what they can for themselves. But this is a multi-layered picture; we are going over information that is very old indeed, which goes back to the primal questions. What is reality? What is existence? Who am I?

These concepts are only consistent with the idea that life is an on-going process of existence. That it is a learning process, which moves the essential being onward, in an ever expanding process of awareness and understanding, and all of the ingredients which go into that are part of that process.

Planetary Karma

On earth there are individual actions being taken, but at the same time there is a way in which those individual actions can be utilised as a group action, the same way in which your bodies individual organs have individual functions but operate as parts of body systems to perform larger functions, and ultimately to function as your physical body.

So you may say, that each individual has their own learning experience, and any group of individuals coming together, may interact to form a group learning experience. Beyond that, any state or government may interact with all these individuals together; to form part of a learning experience which all of them need to have, and therefore, it is initiated as a national experience. It can expand outwards, and yes, you can have a planetary conscious experience, and a series of planetary choices, meaning that all beings on the planet have participated. This does not negate any individual's Karmic or learning experience, but rather becomes a part of it. It is just different levels of the same process.

At this moment you may be wondering if, as a result of a planetary Karmic experience, the planet as a whole suffers from a series of cataclysmic events? Or, if the majority of the planet seems to neglect the survival of the planet and manifests a lack of oxygen or a lack of food, how does this balance for those beings who were aware of this and had made every effort not to have this happen? Why do they have to suffer along with the rest, when they already understood the nature of the lesson, and were working to prevent those results?

1. You will find that they do not suffer quite as much as the rest.

2. You would find that their feeling of not having participated in the act that brought on the disaster, and yet still have to suffer; it is part of their expanding consciousness. One must come to understand the feeling of the innocent, when they become victims of actions that they did not initiate.

3. It is also a very powerful lesson for those who thought nice thoughts, but who took little or no real action.

Now, there is a large proportion of your supposedly conscious community that has sat back and let others take action, or have chosen to talk a great deal, but not actually do anything. So when the inevitable result is experienced, and they say "Yes, but we knew. We recycled our garbage," they may be forced to examine the many things they did not do. The actions that they did not take, the words that they did not speak to the neighbours down the street. These are also part of the learning experience.

Within a community, whenever an experience takes place, there is always a place of refuge. There are always places where those who are conscious can establish protection for themselves. You have areas in different countries, and indeed whole countries, preserving a small ecosystem. Maintaining a small population within a controlled area, can be done in many countries. It is now being done in parts of North America, Australia and New Zealand to name a few. Other places will not be so fortunate. That is the nature of planetary experience.

It is difficult to envision living through a cataclysmic event, like the destruction of a significant portion of the planet such as a nuclear accident of some kind, or perhaps the impact of a space body, or similar event. Once again, you have to trust that you have already grown past certain experiences.

The choice not to destroy the planet through the use of nuclear weapons was made[13], and has been maintained. Regardless of the many conflicts, which may break out, and the many dangers of other types of nuclear accidents, the threat of wholesale destruction of the planet through nuclear war, has been eliminated. The choice was made! And you can see the results of that choice every day. No matter how frightening situations get, there are certain things that are not happening.

Now, that doesn't mean that an effective force of destruction cannot exist in other ways, but that particular choice, because it became that real, and because the planet wide consciousness of all persons was raised enough, that choice was made and has been acted upon.

Karma is a process of education, not a process of retribution. It is not a punishment, but unfortunately it has been made to seem that way. It has also become a refuge for those who need to believe that they will get back something, or that someone who has done them

---

13 *This decision was made through the mass consciousness during the Harmonic Convergence in August 1987*

wrong will be punished. So if it is comforting for one to believe that, let them believe it. It is not conscious, but it is comforting.

There are few who perceive their consciousness, and awareness, as a comforting force, instead of passively resting in the seeming bliss of ignorance. Again that is the difference which separates the conscious being from the semi-conscious one.

By separating, again, we do not make a judgement; it is not a matter of better or worse, only difference. It is the task of forces like myself, to work with those who choose to be conscious.

Healing Therapies

There is a tendency in the practice of "alternative therapies" which bothers me; that of turning a therapeutic tool into the healing source.

I was fortunate to spend a short time studying spiritual thought with a true Master (and I do not use that word lightly) of the healing art, Dennis Adams of Mt Shasta California. He maintains a low profile, and my studies with him were not concentrated on healing, but on the nature of God, the source of all that exists. But, I did learn about healing from him, and have explored that skill from his point of view. The understanding that the source of all healing is not the indiviual healer, nor the crystal, the herb, the colour or sounds themselves, but it is That Which Is God The most important process a being can go through is the understanding of "The Source", everything else will follow naturally as an expression of that understanding.
– M

There are rules that govern the functions of physical reality. The human body, put together as it is, has a physiology, a way of working which is consistent with those rules. Any therapist who finds themselves drawn to an alternative therapy, such as colour healing or magnetic healing, will benefit greatly from understanding the nature of human physiology. Just as a massage therapist during training, learns the directions in which the muscles work, how they are used, and what line to follow to cause them to relax any being who is going to deal with the realignment of the muscle structure, should really study the science of bones, muscles, and ligaments, and the way in which they interact.

The purpose of this section is to clarify that these alternative therapies are additions to the knowledge that exists, not necessarily a substitution. They should be just as disciplined a series of practices as any eight year university medical course – whether or not it takes you eight years depends on your own mentality. Although there is medical knowledge that a natural therapist does not need to have, an advanced course in anatomy and physiology should be part of the basic training of any therapist, regardless of what form of therapy they wish to practice.

Those who would be most blessed by the utilisation of alternative therapies would be those medical practitioners who have come to realise that these are sciences which can be used to enhance their profession. Those who have become most effective in communicating this information are those physicians who have recognised this, and have begun to use these other sciences as part of their training in surgery or other medical procedures.

The purpose of medical sciences and natural therapy sciences has always been to encourage humanity to maintain its most perfect natural health. It is only logical and therefore inevitable, that they join forces in this common goal, in service to human kind.

Meditation

Meditation is the process of placing the body in a state of relaxation to allow different events to take place, while the mind remains conscious of those events. Meditation occurs on a wide range of frequencies and levels, very similar to the levels of sleep that the body goes through as it descends into deeper and deeper sleep. Sometimes these meditations are given names, but meditation by itself is simply the relaxing of the body to a point where you can access a frequency in your mind which is normally inaccessible while the body is active.

Meditative activity at the most basic level is what you call relaxation techniques. The mind is taken on a fantasy journey, which is very similar to the kind of dream fantasy that anyone with an active imagination might set up just before they go to sleep, to detach themselves from reality. Thus, the physical body begins to consciously let go of tension, which then allows the mind to roam freely.

During the first stage, the mind usually begins to replay the activities of the day. This is why meditation therapists often take their students on a guided journey. Words or music may be used to distract them from those everyday activities to get them well on the way into an alternative frequency where, at the lowest spectrum, you create visualisations, and at the highest spectrum, you border on dimensional travel.

That is the frequency where you are actually leaving the current realm and sending your spirit body on a journey to experience or witness events that have already occurred, or are occurring in other dimensional spaces. At that point the body may be relaxed prone, relaxed sitting up, or in any posture you wish. The best and most effective postures have to do with a straight spine. Not straight to the point of rigidity, but straight to the point that communication and information to the body and the mind may pass through most effectively.

Meditation is the conscious duplication of the physical actions which take place during sleep, so that you may also duplicate consciously, the internal actions (the spirit actions) that occur naturally in that state. One of those internal actions involves the ability to contact the frequencies at which different communications take place.

These frequencies can relate to channelling, healing, the communication with your microparticular structure, the frequency at which the Soul Body may go travelling, (astral travel frequency), the frequencies at which you contact higher energy, or the frequencies at which you travel through dimensional space. This is what people are referring to when they are speaking of levels.

It is necessary for the body to rest periodically, so that the internal organs may come to the most perfect moment of peace that they can achieve. It is in this moment of peace that healing is most effective. Without this moment of peace the organs cannot initiate the procedures of replication and repair, or cleanse themselves of the toxins of the day.

When a person has a disease, it is often preferred that they remain unconscious, so that healing may take place without disruption. The natural reaction of animals when they are diseased is to rest, to remain quiet as much as possible, or to sleep.

When a body is diseased, there is a natural tendency to feel tired – this is because so much is going on internally. It is your body's way of saying "Do us a favour, stay down, stay relaxed, and let us do what we must do." Consequently, persons who tend to over exert themselves beyond what is healthy, often manifest illness to cause them to relax!

Those people who meditate deeply and more regularly may find that they need less sleep. This is a natural side effect of meditation; in fact you can completely eliminate the need for sleep through meditation. Your body still requires the same rest it would achieve in the deepest sleep, but this can be achieved through the deepest meditation. Meditation, even for a short period, everyday, on a regular basis, can achieve the same allowance for the body to cleanse and repair itself, as would normally be achieved during several hours of deep sleep.

Meditation is a process which contributes to the overall extension of life force. This is the goal of meditation and the thing that must be achieved if you're going to exist totally without sleep. Needless to say, it is difficult to achieve this state when you are surrounded by activities, which work in contradiction to the state required. In order to achieve the deepest sleep you must feel perfectly secure. Most sleeping disorders are caused by either thought processes that will not quieten down, or a sense of not being safe, which prevents you from falling into the deepest sleep.

Meditation is a process of frequency. Different levels may be achieved according to your own discipline, your effectiveness and what you are trying to accomplish.

Meditation can also be used in conjunction with a series of physical movements such as Tai Chi, which are usually designed to provide a distraction from mental chaos. If you are focusing on following the teacher then all of your movements and thoughts are on that, and this by itself takes you away from distracting thoughts, and sets up a series of physical flows, which begin to centre and focus your energy.

You may follow this activity, with stillness (being in a comfortable relaxed posture, and remaining still) allowing the flow of movement to take you into relaxation. This allows a much deeper level of meditation than is ordinarily accessed, but you must give yourself the time. There cannot be a concern about how long the class lasts and what you have to do afterwards.

Needless to say, the care you take in the maintenance of your physical form will have a direct bearing on the preservation of the deepest meditation in your body. For example, the fewer toxins your organs have to clear the less time they need to clear them. The more relaxed your everyday life, and the fewer pollutants you put into it, the more at peace your body will be with yourself. This is again only logical.

Meditation is therefore, the act of physical relaxation, at the same time that the mind is allowed to access different frequencies of vibration, according to the depth of the relaxation and the purpose required by the meditation.

Many people will discover that they can achieve a level of frequency for the purpose of communication or healing, while the body is still relatively active. They may ask how they can be at this deep frequency and still be aware of their body reacting internally to the passage of gas or liquids, and the sounds around them even though their muscle structure is relaxed.

The first thing that relaxes is the muscle structure, but to relax the internal organs is a step into another frequency, and most beings do not attempt that. It comes very close to sleep and many people who begin a meditation will fall asleep as they go deeper. It is as if they achieved the frequency where certain relaxation takes place and their conscious mind automatically does what it always does when it gets that relaxed. Turns off!

Some teachers, although very well meaning, teach without fully understanding or explaining the process. In many cases students are not being brought back properly from the depth of frequency they were in, and are going out into the world without being completely present. This often happens because a time limit has been set.

People are not all the same, they cannot be brought back within the same time, in the same way. The teacher at that point is trying to be aware of this, but they are also aware that the next class is waiting to come in. So as often as they tell their students not to go out until they are capable, the person themselves may feel pressured, or they may be feeling capable before they are ready.

You know very well that if you have been accessing a certain frequency and you have not tuned yourself down, you are wide open to receive and respond to the many divergent energies that are existing around you. So, many people are opening themselves up to the radiating thought patterns of other beings without realising it. They are reacting to emanating electromagnetic fields, that they were not sensitive to previously. Consequently, illnesses, bacterium, and all sorts of things are having a wonderful time, penetrating through energy fields that are supposed to be relaxed and in some protective energy.

Relaxation takes place from the outside in. The outer structures and the muscles relax first, and then it goes inwards, deeper and deeper. Well, the returning process is supposed to occur in the reverse order. First you activate the inner structures and then you slowly emerge outwards. But when the process is not being done with full time, the muscle structures are activated and functioning before the internal workings have returned to normal.

You should reverse the procedure you followed going into the meditation, and take it a step at a time. Your body should not be moving until every single internal structure is working up to normal functioning speed. That means that the mind is fully there and conscious, way before the body begins to move.

When the body has begun to move again, you take time to let it coordinate its actions with the internal structures. A proper meditation should never have a deliberate physical activity planned for immediately after it. This is why there is that automatic process of everyone having a chat and a cup of tea, or whatever – it helps. A meditation where the body has not come fully back is not really doing the job. Almost the same amount of time you have been in the meditation should be taken to come out of it, before you actually perform any other activity.

A morning meditation is very different, where an energising effect is sought. You have just emerged from sleep, so you do not need to relax the body. Instead you begin the process of energising the body – by focusing the mind on the chakra[14] points – and the energy frequencies to send light flowing through it. It is less of a meditation than the focusing of mental energy.

That is why so many morning meditations involve physical activity, as in forms such as the Salute to the Sun[15]. You can use physical meditation to generate activity, but again, in any such case you finish off with breathing and a unification of your energy. If the breathing is deep, forceful and strong, you feel that surge as you get up and you move slowly into your day, waiting for all frequencies to attune themselves into the space you need to be in to confront your day.

[14] The word "Chakra" comes from the Sanskrit word for "wheel" or "circle". They are vortices' of energy which are located along the body from the base of the spine to the top of the head and which pass through the body from front to back. They are most often referred to in the healing practices and spiritual philosophies of Eastern and Oriental cultures, and can vary in number from four to eleven according to the particular teaching. The position of the chakra point on the body is usually associated with the characteristics of that area and with a colour. Hermeas will discuss chakras in detail in the next book - M

[15] A series of yogic postures designed to activate the entire body at the beginning of the day.

People who begin a regular practice of meditation find their lifestyles changing, because they cannot live the lifestyle they were living before and perform regular meditation. The body does not want to be in that same frequency of activity. People who are determined to do both find themselves in extreme disruption. But that is rarely the case, because any being who has undertaken a course of meditation, even to a superficial level, will find themselves changing their lifestyle.

It is inevitable!

HEALING MODALITIES

Chiropractic

The whole science of Chiropractic was considered a quack therapy for many years, as you know; even though studies, for most chiropractors, are just as intensive as for some doctors. Chiropractic, practised properly, incorporates natural therapies, herbs, the breathing in of certain smokes, acupressure, and should incorporate acupuncture (although that has recently been added through the unity between East and West).

It is part of the orthopaedic sciences, and utilises the movement and adjustment of bone structure, ligament and muscle structure, to allow the body to keep the spine correct. This allows messages to flow freely through the body to cause the perfect communication, which leads to perfect health.

With maintenance, the body will last much longer and there will be fewer problems. When a problem does occur, medical science is there to deal with it. To deal with a problem that you have already done everything you can to avoid. It is simply that humanity has a tradition of avoiding responsibility and allowing someone else to tell them what to do.

Colour Therapy

Colour is a property of light; a vibrational frequency interpreted by your brain. Colour is registered through a process which involves the reflection of light, whether it is the colour of your shirt, or a piece of material that is reflecting light in a certain vibratory frequency.

The essence of colour healing, in the physical sense, has always been the use of coloured light. All such things are based on the mind and if you are going to use colour to heal the auric and the physical bodies, it must be within the visible spectrum.

Colour healing is essentially working with the auric field, which is most responsive to colour and gives off shadings of it in response to emotional situations. Colour can repair and heal the body, when the frequency of the colour aligns with the emotion needed to activate the microparticulars, so healing can take place.

An effective application of this methodology is spectro-chromatics[16], which involves the measuring of light frequencies, and using coloured slides (glass or theatrical gels) of the appropriate frequency, in conjunction with a light, which can then be directed at the body.

Thus, when you have a heat burn, and you focus a blue light of the appropriate frequency on that burn it will stimulate a healing reaction. It is not that cold has suddenly been applied, but the counteracting of a heat red, being balanced by the application of cold blue, which takes the message of heat red away from the cells in that section. The cells are basically being told that they are not

---

[16] *The system of colour therapy known as Spectra-Chrome was introduced by Dinshah Ghadiali. The term is used here because I am familiar with it. However, Herméas is referring to a therapeutic form which is not exactly the same thing. More information on Spectra Chromography as a therapy may be found at, http://www.wrf.org/news/news0004.htm, and in the book Let There be Light by Darius Dinshah – M*

burned; and being extremely responsive, may be willing to accept that.

That is how light healing works. It is a viable healing form, and everyone should know about it, and have a collection of coloured slides. It is like having aspirin in your medicine cabinet. It is something you should have on hand to be used with an understanding of how it works. Of course one must acquire some understanding, just as any mother acquires information on first aid and what to do in the case of an insect bite or poisoning. There are some people who will take the time to find these things out and some who will not.

There are dietary philosophies involving the taking into the body of certain coloured foods (red and orange foods, yellow foods, green foods) for the colour effect. This is a misunderstanding of what is happening. Colour in foods is related to their natural mineral and chemical content; the colour of a food reflects certain properties. Foods that tend to produce reds and oranges have certain minerals and nutritional contents, and foods that are green tend to have different contents.

Again we are working with the power of mind, and the influence of the mind's understanding of what is being absorbed (in the case of food in combination with nutritional balance). It is not that such diets do not work, it is just that they do not work for the reason that they are supposedly working. It is not simply the colour, but rather the effects of the minerals, whose presence are indicated by the colour.

Colour is just an indication key, and those nutritional keys have a relationship to the chakra points they are attuned to. So if you eat red and orange food, it is highly probable that they have many mineral contents that relate to the needs of the organs related to the lower chakras. This is not really a great mystery.

Solarised waters[17] also work essentially with the mind and intention – as a focus of that intention. These waters hold the frequency of intention of the colour with which it has been radiated. They give off the essence of the colour, but colour is not transmitted internally in this or any other way. A visual representation of a colour frequency cannot be absorbed internally by ingestion. However, depending on its sensitivity to the concept, a body may or may not respond to the ingesting of solarised water.

You remember we have discussed the nature of the microparticular functions in the body, and how they respond to general intent. The problem with getting these microparticulars to function in alignment with your needs is the lack of focus of human thought. Something as specific as the use of colour, focuses both the mind of the therapist and the mind of the patient on a symbolic representation of a frequency that will trigger the response of the microparticulars, as when your internal organs respond to an influx of vitamin C or iron mineral contents, etc.

In all cases the most efficient form of using colour for healing is the power of the mind to envision the colour, as your mind is the only organ capable of recreating the exact frequency of a healthy auric colour.

Artificial colour formats can only come close within the frequency span, but the mind, using essential colour, can pinpoint the exact frequency. Though once again, we get back into the difficulties involved with the human being focusing a thought, that specifically on a certain area.

---

17 *Water that has been imbued with the properties of a given colour by placing water in a glass container, with a coloured gel around it, in the sunlight.*

The use of colour in visualisation is most effective, and easiest for the amateur to utilise, as colour has a very strong radiating effect on the whole body. Every other form of colour therapy is fundamentally symbolic.

Your thoughts can direct colour into a deeper area, even though light does not function deeply inside the body. It functions on the auric body, which sympathetically sends a communication to specific areas.

So in essence with the use of colour, when you visualise putting the light into an organ, you are not actually putting in light as such, but rather setting off a key to the specific frequency vibration required for healing that organ. You are tuning into the auric relationship to that organ and giving it maximum efficiency. You are communicating an intention to the internal cellular structure. As in the intention of cooling blue against red heat; it is symbolic.

The mind is the only thing that truly heals.

Sound Therapy

Once again we are dealing with frequencies and tonal vibrations. The use of proper tonality can have incredible power over matter of any kind. The use of sound, tonal reproduction in certain patterns and frequencies can cause dimensional transitions and the adjustment of matter in such a way that it can change its density. The Human voice is remarkably flexible and is capable of producing a wider range of tonalities than is commonly realized. However, as you may expect, controlled and effective usage of sound in healing requires considerable study and guidance. Use of naturally produced tonal vibration to alter the physical structure of inanimate matter is a skill the knowledge of which is not currently available to you.

The sound frequencies producible by the human voice, and the sensitivity of individuals who practice tonal healing, are flexible enough that there is little danger of finding an individual whose awareness and abilities are so much in alignment that they can accidentally, without the appropriate training, produce the level of change that the ancient priests and wise ones were able to utilise. In other words, I do not think that someone will go whistling past a ball of granite and cause it to suddenly float away because they have happened to hit the right frequency.[18]

Those who work with sound healing are working in the best way that they can, to duplicate what is a far more effective way of changing physical structure than light healing.

Light works essentially on the auric body, and hints the microparticulars into functioning. The appropriate tone actually communicates with the microparticular structure of the body; it is specific. You can direct a sound into an organ. You can direct a vibration, as in the use of ultrasound and sonics.

This technique is now being used by your medical community to disrupt kidney stones and gall stones, which are being broken up by use of this vibration. This is a mechanical variation on what was once done without the electronics. Therefore, sound healing is actually a far more effective system than light, but the appropriate training is not really available. Some searching would have to be done.

The healing power of music has always been known. The Pythagorean's understood the nature of healing music and the use of certain tones and scales to bring the body to rest. Every human being practices this art to a degree, as you play your relaxing

18 *The Maori of New Zealand have a long tradition of making heavy objects light by chanting, though there are few alive who can do this now. – E*

meditative music, and each of you finds music most suited to you, to create a certain sensation. The use of sound to effect human spirit and physical health is not new. The next step is to apply the specifics of using it to actually address parts of the body.

Cancer can be completely cured by the use of the appropriate tone. A cancer in the body (the replication of cells unnecessarily) is an imbalance in vibrational structure. The appropriate tones can completely inhibit this, and indeed cause it to regress. You might say you would give the cancer an earache and it will retreat. A tumour can be easily broken up by the application of the appropriate sound wave. It can be dissolved, or shaken loose. It is known that sound at a certain frequency can break a glass, so why cannot sound at a certain frequency disrupt a clot of fleshy matter?

This is the direction that medical science is moving in, which is of course, going back to what was already known.

Singing bowls and playing instruments within the aura

Crystal bowls and even brass bowls produce a wide range of very penetrating vibrations; they are like tuning forks. They would take up a lot more room, but a series of bowls tuned to frequencies of eighths would be deeply effective. This is why they are used to create a meditative vibration.

Another frequency sound that is very powerful is the Aboriginal wooden instrument. The didgeridoo creates a very powerful tonal vibration, and that vibration amplifies and uses the human voice. Thus, tools are used to create what is not there – frequency and depth of penetration. One might also use a series of wooden flutes, tuned to eighth tones to produce a similar effect.

Instruments came into being to create the vibrational frequencies that were beyond the human voice's ability to create, but the ability to penetrate with that sound is not always there. Again these devices can be misused. The use of certain tonalities, especially in the use of crystal or brass gongs and bowls, can be disruptive to some beings.

Those who are dedicated to a practice that uses these in their everyday work may refuse to acknowledge the disruptive effect on another being. Not everyone is tuned to the same note, and any who forced themselves to be surrounded by vibrations that were not bringing them joy would be, in essence, making themselves ill. It is known that certain sound frequencies and decibel levels of sound are extremely destructive to the body and the spirit, but this knowledge is not being applied.

Everything we are speaking of can be proven; it has a factual basis, and is not spiritual speculation. Researchers already know this to be true. They simply haven't taken it to its farthest extension, because when they do, it takes them into the realms of the as yet, unproven, and humankind gets extremely nervous with that. Especially when the extensions are being proposed by those who do not have a scientific degree, to indicate they have a right to think such thoughts. It is not that the information cannot be verified. It can. But the testing methods currently being applied by scientific researchers in these fields are not designed to allow for certain types of results. Unexpected answers to scientific examinations are often rejected as contaminated testing or mere anomalies.

However our point is the information gets out sooner or later. And eventually, testing methodology will undergo its own evolution to allow for these types of understandings.

Crystal Healing

Crystals do not heal. They have never healed. They cannot. A crystal is a tool. It is a device that has certain essential functions.

There are crystals which are repositories of information, and their job is to act as a library, to take in and give out information. Crystals which do that have no other purpose. They will have natural properties which all crystals have. They will vibrate when struck, and they will bend light if they have certain angles in them. These are the natural properties of all crystals.

Another function is amplification. There are crystals, which are designed, in and of themselves, to magnify or direct vibration in some way. This may be thought vibration, it may be light, it may be sound, etc.

As you work with a crystal you can tune it to a specific purpose. In most cases, those who use crystals to heal are amplifying their intention, their thought. They may think they are putting a colour through, they may feel they are putting a sound through, and some aspect of that colour or sound may actually pass through, but essentially they are sending a thought. The thought is amplified by the crystal and directed to where it is supposed to go.

To place crystals arbitrarily on the chakras of the body is symbolic of intent. No crystal by itself has a function. It is a tool exclusively. There are those who use crystals very actively in their healing and psychic practices. If they believe the crystal to have sentience, (a property of intelligence, of individuality) they have made an error in judgement.

It is possible that they are dealing with a communication crystal. Communication can be another function of crystal, as it is related to the amplification of vibration. Crystal can be specifically tuned to one particular frequency of information and establish a link between one self and another. Now sometimes one might misunderstand and think that the crystal is talking to them; but this is not so.

Crystal does not speak. It is however, a communication device and may be spoken through. Under certain circumstances it may suit the interests of communicator to not be specific as to the source of the information being given, so an assumption that it originates from the crystal would not be corrected. It is also true that when a being is receiving information from a crystal (that is to say taking back recorded information) it may seem to come out in language, and therefore resemble direct communication.

Consequently, if you use crystals in healing, they are simply the focus of your own intent. If they serve you, so be it, but they are no more nor less necessary than anything else. Crystals with a specific colour can only enhance your efforts if you are using them in conjunction with colour, but the crystal has its own vibrational frequency of that colour. For example, there are many different shades of purple and violet within stones that produce that colour. In addition to the colour, there are many individual properties that belong to these stones.

Due to the wide range of oranges, of reds, of blues, of purples, of greens, on the planet the designations for colour are once again only symbolic of intent.

The age of crystal use is still in its infancy. There has been a flurry of activity around them, but again it was based on much ignorance of the true essence of how crystals are used. You now have a whole bunch of people walking around with wide ranges of crystals, using them with only moderate effect. The number of crystals you have makes absolutely no difference to the kind of work you are doing.

If you happen to live in a place that has large exposed crystals all around, you should be aware of disruptive frequency energy, which is created by the amplification of electromagnetic energy. Crystals bounce light and pick up sounds, so the more sensitive you are, the more aware you must be. That is why certain crystals can be with you in certain spaces and others cannot. As in all things, quantity is not the important factor.

Crystals have a function, and when they have performed that function they may be let go, or if they have an ongoing function they may stay to perform it. Crystals tend to go where they must, to be with whoever they must be with, but this is governed by universal intent and understanding, rather than by the crystals themselves. It is similar to the energy fields that bring a home to you or financial abundance if they are in alignment with your life plan.

Properties within crystals, which deal with different organs in the body are related to colour and symbolism. Once again there has been confusion as to how healing takes place. Most of the vitamins and many minerals existing inside the body are in crystalline format; they are organically a part of everything. Hence, one can say that crystals affect parts of the body, because lack or over dominance of certain crystalline structures can cause imbalance within the body. And by adding that crystalline structure, or taking something to leach some of it away, the body can be brought back into balance.

So in that sense, some properties of crystals are very much a part of the human being. But a physical crystal structure existing externally does not suddenly penetrate and affect the body. Again, it is the focus of intent. Thus, if you wear a carnelian, it will not affect your liver with the magic associated with stones. Focus of the mind is required for healing to occur. You would find that there is very little understanding between the reality of the world of the crystal, and the human.

I do not want to complicate this issue by getting into the vibrational dimension wherein crystals interact with each other, because again this relates to the microparticular structure, and levels of intelligence and awareness that exist in other dimensional realities. Those who work with crystal in the art of healing, communication or in any other way may not understand how they are interacting with those types of worlds, but that is a different subject.

Herbalism

I do not really consider herbalism an alternative tool. It is, and has been truth for aeons. All medical forms that you have today are a derivative of natural medicines, which come from plants and other life forms natural to this planet; of which herbs are only one form. All plant structures have properties, and those properties can affect a human body in a helpful way, or in a poisonous way. The study of those properties is a viable study and again should be the inheritance of every human being. There should be an understanding of the use of certain plants and herbs for immediate healing purposes. It depends on the activity of the human whether they are going to take the time and energy to explore them. There is no question about the validity of herbalism at all. The questions of validity are related to the practitioners or the producers of herbal derivatives in your various cultures.

The effect of herbalism is direct and physical. In fact, of the subjects we have discussed the most direct physical response in the human body would be to an herbal tea or the herb itself. Needless to say those most freshly accessed have the greatest properties. The study of herbal lore is extremely effective for healing.

In most cases, medicines are simply concentrated versions of the same thing. It is when they are artificially produced that humans begin to interfere with the properties and problems may occur. They do not realise that the individual property which they have concluded is the one which affects a particular illness, must be balanced by other properties in the herb, which keep the healing factor from becoming dangerous to the body. Hence the cure sometimes becomes more dangerous than the disease.

Aromatherapy

Like herbs, aromatherapy is a very effective therapy, because certain fragrances can affect the mind and spirit – in the same way in which music is applied. Certain music will have tonal adjustments within it, which will have an effect on the human body and spirit. The same applies to fragrances. You will not cure cancer with a scent. You can however, induce the body into a more appropriate state to initiate healing, with a scent. You can create an environment more conducive for communication with the microparticular function with scent.

Aromatherapy is just that, it is the smell of the oil. To call the application of a scented oil to the bottom of the feet, aromatherapy, is a misnomer; unless you are planning to smell your feet. This position where the foot is drawn up to the nose is not the most effective way of relaxing the foot [laughter]. Therefore, to sell people a wide variety of back rubbing oils, which have properties in them of other oils, is ineffective unless the scent of those oils is so powerful that it will permeate the room. The smell of an oil placed upon a muscle does not relax the muscle; the smell must be registered through the nose. The lingering scent of massage oil which has been used on a body can have a beneficial effect in that manner, but not in a direct way as is sometimes implied.

So it would be far more effective to use an oil burning pot if you are going to use aromatherapy. When you have put onto the body a large quantity of certain oil combinations, which have a specific and strong scent, there will be a very subtle odour, and that may assist a process. But essentially aromatherapy is within the realm of scent, those smells which affect the body. It is also true that the oils of certain plants have different properties, but those properties are extremely subtle and in the quantities that you are currently using them, are negligible. Again it has become a misunderstanding of a very ancient science, which has also been turned into a commercial prospect.

Hands On Healing

There are several forms vital to the understanding of healing; hands on healing, vibrational healing, miracle healing. Reiki, is one popular method, utilising Ki energy There is also another energy being used, which is a variation on the use of Ki energy. Both of these methods involve the opening up of awareness to frequency vibrations, wherein the human body becomes a channel for the very natural and balanced healing energy, which is organic to the planetary structure.

Essentially the energy is used to bring a physical body, which is out of balance, (in dis-ease) back into tune with the natural healing environment. The healing process can be sped up, depending on the strength and focus energies directed to an individual, and that individual's willingness to allow and accept the healing. They activate, and boost the natural process of healing in the body.

Although when there is damage, which requires a more specific or a more aggressive approach, the energy can really do nothing more than create a more beneficial environment for healing.

The instantaneous healings of Jesus Christ were not confined to the use of Ki energy alone. It was combined with other understandings, which included the manipulation of matter and the great power of connection with the *Ultimate Creative Force*. This allowed the instantaneous reformation and recreation of whatever is required, and the removal of what is not.

Thus, the blind see. How does this occur? It is quite simple. You dissolve the inefficiently functioning cellular structure, and consciously rebuild it instantly, because you are one with *That Which Is The Creator*, which is what a Christ is. In order to achieve this, the physical body must be aligned, in complete openness to healing. This enables the natural healing energy to bring the body back to complete health, and allows instantaneous transformation to occur more easily, because it is accepted, the body knows it is correct, and it is done! **All hands heal!**

However those who are born open to a healing energy, or who have a history of it in their family will find the energy flows more easily, as will those who have taken a course, or have worked with a specific energy. And those who have it in their background, will have learned techniques from their family, which may or may not, place limitations on their understanding of what they are capable of doing – how the polarities of different hands work, etc.

There are three frequency channels for healing energy. Reiki encompasses two at different levels. The third one is used by other beings in other dimensions, but can be accessed by human beings (sometimes they are stumbled upon) as well.

All healing energies come through the body via the hands. Some healers, who do not understand what they are doing, sometimes take the healing energy into their body and then they push it out.

Thus, it actually comes from them. It is still passing through, but they are acting as a middle man, and in this way they can exhaust themselves.

Some people tap into the third line of healing energy so strongly that they experience the sensation of taking onto themselves the illness of the person they are healing, and processing the healing within themselves. It is not the other being who heals themselves, or is healed, but rather the illness is removed from them and in an empathetic manner. The healer then takes the diseasement into their body and processes the healing through themselves, which can be very strenuous. It is more effective to have all three avenues wide open, and use a combination of any of them.

Sometimes, an individual who needs healing has been so debilitated by the illness that it is difficult for them – even once the body has received permission to be in the most conducive state for healing – to allow healing to take place. When a client is already experiencing a sense of defeat, the healer can, by using that third frequency, literally remove some of the disease into their own very healthy format and allow their own energy to heal it. They heal the illness within themselves, instead of it simply being healed by passing the energy through.

When this technique is required, it is important that the healer understands that a conscious choice must be made. It requires an opening of empathy, sensation, and body, mind and spirit, to the other being, and is closely related to the understanding of the nature of the *Creative Force*.

Your Master Teachers who perform instantaneous healing, have all three of these conduits wide open, in addition to the manipulation of matter, which is a separate energy. The manipulation of matter is not directly connected with healing; but can be used in that process. They are different fields altogether, which is why the miracle of the instantaneous healing is so very rare. In some cases, what seems to be instantaneous, or rather miraculous, is often connected to the acceptance of the individual who is receiving the healing, aggressively participating in the healing process.

There are some cases where even the most powerful focus of vibrational healing does not seem to work. This is further proof that healing is something that one gives permission for, and must be acceptable in the overall life plan of the individual. Otherwise the vibrational healing can do nothing more than comfort and bring a certain peace.

One, who understands the manipulation of matter and the use of the empathetic healing, can even bypass the pattern of a person's life and cause instantaneous healing. But if the pattern is required by that person, they will simply recreate the illness again, or something else will take its place. This has been seen so many times. It is very sad, is it not? There is a limit to what you can do to repair damage that is done, if the situation is such that those beings must experience that damage.

Regression Therapy

There is so much confusion about the nature of past lives, living on this planet, and the nature of incarnation. It is amazing how this material has been complicated.

The experiences of all beings exist in the ether, and a person can tune into any experience and decide that it was their own. The fastest way to learn, and accomplish great wisdom in one lifetime is to tune into the widest range of experiences that other beings have had, and borrow. The more attuned you become to another beings experience, the more you feel as if it is happening to you. It is simply a way to speed up the educational process! It is real, but only real in that moment.

Most people have not been who they think they have been in the course of searching out past lives; and unfortunately most past life therapists would not know the difference between tapping into a frequency of information, and actually going back to a past life. In fact people have not lived quite as many lives as they think they have.

Sometimes they confuse a life experience from another planet, with a life experience on this planet, or they are confused by one of the existences of the planet during the three previous ages when the planet has been returned to minimal existence.

You never grasp the entire aspect of the past; you catch glimpses – like an interrupted signal. The only time past life regression is effective or purposeful, is when you have carried aspects of a previous life into this lifetime. Under these circumstances it is helpful to go back and resolve or reprogram in some way. That is the only time that it has significance.

Within the cellular structure of your physical body, is the memory of events that have already occurred in this lifetime and sometimes in a past lifetime, if those events were not properly completed. When you are dealing with the healing of a mind or a spirit, it is important to scan the body for signals, which would indicate that there is a memory pattern of an action within the body. This requires that you be tuned specifically to the frequencies of the cellular level.

We have already discussed scanning the body for the use of colour and sound, but these are different frequencies. The section of the body that has a cellular memory of an abuse – whether in this lifetime or another – will have a colour pattern attached to it. It will also have a sound vibration. But if you apply a colour or sound adjustment, it may or may not be effective in dealing with that memory. It might bring the body back to balance but it will still shake itself loose, and become untuned again. In this case, you would have to be aware that there is information to be dealt with.

Those who are tuned to the science of psychic and spirit healing would then read the information to find out what is held within the cellular memory of the specific part of the body. If it is in this lifetime, then a regression therapy can be utilised. Regression therapy is the taking of the individual into the past of this lifetime, using hypnosis.

The best way to approach regression is to get the person in the state of relaxation and move them back slowly through time. Then the therapist must bring forward the memory of that body structure, and tune the individual to it. Once this is achieved, the therapist then asks the individual to go back to the place where the event took place, and recite what they are experiencing, or to feel it once again.

If you are in this lifetime you are dealing with the soul embodiment and physical body created in this lifetime. It simply means that the action taken to generate a lesson that had to be learned created such an extreme emotional response that the lesson could not be fully absorbed. It was felt, but not adjusted to.

So you take them back to that emotional response from their current perspective, to absorb the lesson required from that experience, thereby releasing the emotional trauma associated with it.

You are healing the Soul Body, which is created for the purpose of holding emotion. There is an imbalance in the Soul Body, a flaming hotspot, as it were, and this method assists the absorption of information and puts in its proper place – which restores balance. If the hotspot has been affecting the physical behaviour of the person, that behaviour should change. Sometimes this can be accomplished without the process of regression or hypnotic trance, simply remembering the emotional response and the telling of it, can accomplish the same thing.

When dealing with a past life you are essentially doing the same thing, except you are crossing into a dimensional past. One technique of regression is to proceed, using the same technique, to the moment where an event occurred in the past life, and replay it exactly as it existed. In this case you are working with the spirit embodiment, which does not feel emotion, the soul is feeling, but it is the Essential Spirit that has not received the information. So the soul has been carrying and replaying this emotional burden because the transmission was garbled and not absorbed.

With regression, the Soul Body, without the physical body, remembers and re-experiences the emotions associated with the action at the time, and is therefore able to receive the lesson. The spirit immediately assimilates the lesson, and at that moment the emotional memory ceases to have any power. This is very effective, because the experience in that lifetime was created for generating the emotion which taught a specific lesson.

Another technique is interchange therapy, where you completely change that experience into something else, so that it no longer affects the current body. Having taken the person back to what actually occurred in the other lifetime, the therapist then attempts to change what occurred.

Now this gets a bit more complicated, which is why it often doesn't work. There are individuals who find this technique very effective for themselves, but they do not realise that this is because they have become very facile at going from one dimensional path to another. However, trying to impose the same technique onto another who may not be so comfortable with shifting dimensions is more difficult.

It would be far better to take the individual back to the real past where the problem occurred, have them remember it, and then bring them back to the present. Once back in the present, you tell them to go to an alternative past where the situation is different. If you then, consciously take them back to that other past, you will have a better chance of changing the experience of the event.

The question then becomes – will they have to recreate something similar to learn the lesson that was unlearned? In the process of going back to experience what actually occurred, they have given the information to the spirit body. It is simply that there has been emotional residue left over, and in order to clear that, they then change what has occurred, so that there is no emotional residue. By the simple act of going back and reading the emotional memory, the Essential Spirit has immediately absorbed the lesson that had to be learned. Usually it is a very traumatic experience, as one rarely carries with one the physical psychic memory of an event of a joyous nature.

The technique for going into an alternative past should be used by individuals on themselves. It is possible to have truly absorbed and understood a lesson but a residue of emotion remains due to the power of the experience. In that event, the individual themselves, in the act of relaxation, meditation or even sleep, may choose to go back to a different past, with the same characters and change the situation to be more of that which they require to cleanse all emotional residue.

Then, if they wish, they can bring that alternative past into their past timeline. So that it becomes part of their current present. The original event then becomes more like a fantasy or dream. There is no problem with this, as long as they are living very much in the present, because it becomes only one of the miscellaneous pasts that has gone into dreamland. It no longer has a real or powerful effect.

It is more difficult to change when the past is still affecting the present, because it is a matter of denying that an event took place, and that does not solve any problems. It is the same as when people have forgotten or chosen to block out an event. We know that doesn't work, and eventually the suppressed event emerges. When this happens it is necessary to heal an element of the soul embodiment which is reflecting itself in the physical body.

Psychic Healing

It is possible for a therapist of strong mind to communicate with the microparticulars of another human being to cause rapid healing, by directing the functioning of the microparticulars. You would call this a psychic healing which may be done in direct contact with the human being or through indirect contact.

There are not that many individuals who have the power of mind, direction or the fine focus for such a thought. The original concept behind voodoo dolls and other such external paraphernalia to represent an individual was, for the purpose of healing; not for the purpose of destruction.

To focus the psychic healing power of the healer, a replica of the person needing healing was created with some part of their embodiment, which carried a bit of their life essence –usually clippings of hair or nails. The reason these were used is because they still have living energy in them even when they are cut These clippings were placed into the figure and the focus of healing was placed on the part of the figure corresponding to the area afflicted.

If mending was needed, then sewing was performed, if cooling was needed, then cool could be applied to the area. It was a focus for the psychic energy. But as in so many cases, the power to heal was turned into the power to harm, and consequently, people had to build up defences and walls against this type of psychic manipulation.

So. Do voodoo dolls work? Yes, they do. But there are a number of conditions involved, and it is symbolic and a representation of what was once a focus for psychic healing.

The soul embodiment can feel pain and the human being equates pain with diseasement and hence the pain must be removed, because pain cannot be correct. Pain is of course the logical response to something which has occurred and it is a warning signal. So it is correct, in regard to what it is and it must be dealt with. You, (Elizabeth) may deal with your own pain quite effectively. Your pain is a recognition of an injury to your physical body which has not yet been repaired. But to not have that pain, if the physical injury was still there, would be far more dangerous, and very much detrimental to the body

The function of psychic healing, if it is being done correctly, is the fundamental manipulation of the microparticular function. But in some cases the psychic healer simply contacts the aspects of the body that handle pain and its relief, and enhances their actions.

Consequently the individual will feel much better, but the actual act of healing has not taken place.

It is again the focus of intent. Focus, focus, the word is focus! The focus of a thought, the focus of the intent and its effect on the microparticular structures of the body and their response to it.

Magnetic Healing

The body and all things of the Earth have an electromagnetic field. An individual's electromagnetic field has a relation-ship to the planetary electromagnetic field, and that planetary electromagnetic field, has a relationship to the solar magnetic field and of course, to the other planets. These are a succession of energies, and they all have relationship to each other.

Thus, when your sun experiences solar flares or sun spots, which cause outward imbalanced explosions of electromagnetic energy, they immediately affect your planetary energy, causing wonderful distortions to microwave technology and computers, etc. Also those human beings who are sensitive to these fields will find themselves feeling a bit disrupted, under very high energy solar activity.

Working with magnetic fields is similar to working with light healing energy. There are different frequencies of magnetic energy, and working with the kind of magnetic energy that is produced by a metallic object – whose electrons are coaxed into going into the same direction – is not the quite the same thing as working electromagnetic magnetic fields.

In the case of healing, these are techniques which are being remembered, but not deeply understood. Therefore they are not really being used as accurately as they might be. Magnetic jewellery, for example, does not really have the same effect as an electromagnetic field magnet being focused on a specific area of the body.

It is true that a magnet worn in that area of chronic pain may cause relief, by communicating with the microparticular structures in that area and causing them to respond to the flow of the field. But it is very general, and it is actually the focus of the human mind and the intention of the desired effect, that participates in the healing.

In science, and in your new medical technologies, they are rediscovering the use of a magnetic field similar to the way laser beam has a relationship to light. A fine focus stream of electrons, dealing in a magnetic field, directed internally to a specific part of the body, the way you would use injection surgery, it can disrupt a malignancy or cause a focusing of healing in that area, they are also using, an electromagnetic field in the way in which you use ultrasound technologies, yet it is far more effective than ultrasound, in dissolving particles that are foreign to the body by disrupting the electromagnetic fields, which hold them together.

What holds things together? What is your basic understanding of science and physics? You are all going to have to go back to school. I warn your readers that it is time to remember all the things you told your teachers in high school you would have no use for, because you weren't planning to use it as you grew up. You need to know this, because if you understand the process it will be easier for you to implement it.

Electrons have a charge, they have an electromagnetic field. They are brought together or forced apart by that field. Thus, if you focus a stream of magnetic energy of a specific charge at an object (even if it is a fleshy object, a living cell object) you can cause disruption to the electrons which bind substances together. Is this not logical?

Eventually they will discover this, as they learned to use lasers, not only in internal surgery, but for actually cutting. They will create and use a Magnetic Electron Laser, in order to cause an incision and to work, as with a light laser, on the adjustment and the removal of body substances.

Magnetic therapy; is different to magnetic medicine. Magnetic medicine is the use of a magnetic electron field or beam, focused in a specific area, to cause certain effects to occur. Magnetic therapy – the use of magnets in general on the body – is like light therapy, a general influence strongly assisted by the focus of the mind of both the therapist and the recipient. It is no more nor less effective than coloured light therapy, and it is deeply affected by the power and focus of the therapist and the recipient.

It is far better for your current level of therapist, as opposed to trained medical personnel; to continue to work with general all purpose magnets, rather than encouraging them to make their own electron magnet.

In Conclusion

In the end there is only one healing, there is only one technique for anything. That is the use of mind or psyche in all things. Everything else is a focus for that psyche and is only a tool. Even hands-on-healing is part of the focus of the psyche. So there is no act that is performed that does not have its roots in the power of your mind, with its ability to focus, isolate, and tune in its various frequencies clearly and cleanly.

You see, your mind is very much like a tuning device, a radio receiver. The use of mind exercises and various techniques are there to help you fine tune your signal. The difference is you are not a mechanical device; you are a device that thinks and produces.

Once you have learned how to fine tune you should be able to heal without the use of the tools. For instance, if you can create such a clear focus of a specific colour in light, blazing in your mind and send it to the auric body of another individual, you should be able to accomplish as much as the actual light itself.

As a colour therapist and esoteric healer, I found this chapter fascinating, and the added understanding of the process gained from this session, assisted my practice a great deal.

There is a powerful lobby within Australia and New Zealand working against the continuance of natural therapies, which would seem to be trying to regulate and control it out of existence. I believe that if we don't start to act more responsibly and create accredited self regulatory bodies, the only people practising alternative therapies in the future, will be doctors and physiotherapists. After all, there is some reason for concern – people are doing weekend workshops and then setting themselves up as practitioners. If we are to become acceptable in the mainstream, we have to take responsibility for what we are doing, take time to learn how the whole system works – not just the little bit we are specialising in.

I have met practitioners who had no knowledge of the chakra system, or the subtle bodies. I have met colour therapists whose knowledge of colour was confined to looking up an ailment in a chart and applying the colours accordingly. Now I'm not saying that all healers fall into this category by any means, but if we are not careful, the medical profession will use those types of instances against us, lump us all under the same banner and throw the baby out with the bath water. It would be far better for us to institute our own regulation than have it thrust upon us. – E

Channelling

I have always found channelling easy to do. My first experience was during a sing-along, prior to meditation in a group led by my first spiritual teacher, Katheryn Hayward. It took me be surprise – there was I, singing along, when I felt an energy seem to enfold me, and I felt a slight detachment in my mind. Suddenly, my singing voice changed, and what came out was deeper, stronger and more beautiful than anything I had ever produced myself. I was not sure what had happened, but in the following years, I learned more about channelling and how to use that "tool".

My most disciplined training in that skill came during my studies with MAFU (a "walkin" spirit teacher whose information profoundly changed my life, and who first told me "The Story" – his version). My work with him taught me more about the nature of channelling.

Channelling is very much a tool to me, not a profession or means of earning a living. The information verbalised through that process is always affected by the human instrument involved, and is meaningless unless the person makes it their own, in their conscious mind. I believe that everyone can learn to use this tool, though some people will find it easier than others. I assure you that it is not a fantasised experience, but is only a use of the mind which today's scientists and psychologists have not yet understood. – M

All channelling whether it be of "councils" or individual entities, represent frequencies of information access. The concept of the "Council of the Nine" and the "Council of the Twelve" is very similar to people going to different special interest libraries with different levels of information[19].

You would not hand an Encyclopaedia Britannica to a 5-year-old child for information access would you? You would give them one suited in language and concepts to their capacity for understanding. Neither would someone looking for information on art or literature go to a biological sciences library. There are different levels of information for different areas of interest and for different capacities of understanding. Akashic records[20] are another level of information that may be accessed, and again, within that library there are several subsections.

Channelled information is directed and censored, not so much in the sense that you may not access it, but in the sense that it is simplified, and on a need-to-know basis. It is a process of reducing it down to the information required and thereby eliminating That which is not absolutely necessary, or, adding colour to the information somewhat, if the person is sophisticated enough to perceive it.

Many books refer to the White Brotherhood, it is a very ambiguous term and refers mostly to that sensation of light energy that one receives when dealing with a particular level. Essentially the

19 *Entities often referred to in channeled books.*
20 *From esoteric tradition, a library containing records of every event that has ever occurred. It is often the Akashic records that are being accessed during past life regression, for example. – E*

White Brotherhood is devoted to personal guidance, healing, the beginning of acceptance of the gates beyond death, and the understanding of the eternal realms and the nature of spirit and wisdom. The White Brotherhood is just a euphemism for a specific frequency that deals with those issues, so it is still on an elementary level. The White Brotherhood is not so much concerned with the overall effect of the race on the planet or the universe as a whole; they deal with the individuals and little groups.

Angel and archangel energies are a little more specific, you don't really have bands of angels. You have angel entities who deal with specific fields of endeavour, information, and with individuals undergoing particular trials, for the purpose of advancing the planet or the race as a whole. Archangels rarely deal with humanity, as they mostly oversee the other angel entities.

It is true that not every individual who is capable of channelling necessarily accesses that level of information. Some individuals will have a specific frequency line all to themselves to facilitate their contacting the frequency of information they are familiar with. So it is not a complete misrepresentation for a being to say "I alone am accessing this source"

However, a council of any kind, or any channelled entity, can be accessed on more than one frequency within a specific series of wavelengths. It is simply that a different channeller would probably have to use another frequency. They might get slightly different information but they would be accessing, the same basic level of information within the same band of frequencies. Tuning is all that is called for.

So it is not misrepresentation for a being to say "I alone am accessing this source". However it is not true that **no one** else can access the information either. It is simply that they would use another frequency. Therefore they will be accessing within the same band of frequencies, the same basic level of information, this is similar to a radio in which you have a whole sequence of frequencies between 103 and 104 megahertz. Depending on the area in which you are located, the same radio signal will be picked up on a slightly different frequency modulation. In addition, different modulations will produce a stronger signal, and the variety and availability of the modulations will determine how "finely tuned in" the signal may become.

The trouble is that **no matter what frequency is being accessed, the information is filtered in some way when it comes out of the mouth of the individual**. It is screened by the personal experience and knowledge of the individual who is channelling. This is always so! The better the channel, the more wide their personal experiences, the broader their understanding and allowance, the purer and more accurate the information is when it comes through.

Not that it is such a big problem, because in most cases the information being accessed is already in alignment with the individual, as in our case for example. We work together and there is a good alignment, because Martha is in alignment with the information as it is accessed and is, for the most part, in agreement with it,[21] so there is little strain and effort in allowing the information to come through. There is some censorship, but not significant enough to effect the essential information. Also, any censorship is acknowledged by both of you, thus it is addressed. The problems arise when the censorship is unacknowledged, either deliberately or through ignorance and innocence.

21 *Being in agreement with the information means that nothing that is coming out violates my ethics, not that I already know everything which is being discussed – M*

There are some truths that a human being will not allow. Truths that would shatter their very understanding of existence or that challenge their upbringing and culture, are often censored out, either by the channeller, or at the level of information being accessed.

Presenting the Information

The answers given to the people who have asked the questions are limited to the capacity of the individual who is channelling, and to the capacity of the questioner to understand the information.

For this reason we would encourage readers to think in terms of opening up to channelling themselves. It is a way for them to recognise their own capacity for growth in the conscious mind. And doing so is the measure by which they will access higher levels of information in the unconscious mind. So they will be able to make their own decisions regarding their actions in this life. Everybody has a right to access the many sources of spiritual information available. However some directed practice, training, and /or experience, is highly recommended.

There are people who seek, who grow themselves, who search out information to make conclusions that they will take responsibility for, and there are those who will follow, who prefer to be led. They do not want to put in the extra effort and do not want to take the extra responsibility that comes with doing it themselves. The resistance to taking direct responsibility for personal growth and ones actions is quite profound.

The reason why channelling has become popular in the New Age movement, is for the purpose of encouraging individuals to realise that they can access this information. It is part of the next phase of the evolutionary process – allowing into your everyday life, the senses and skills that are yours by birth, but which have been shut down through conscious or unconscious choice.

Healing by the laying on of hands or the use of mind is another example of a channelled frequency, which is the natural right of every human being and which is now undergoing a resurgence of acceptance.

The ultimate goal of the channeller is the using of frequencies to **instantly** access the widest possible range of information in order to confront any situation that arises.

Unfortunately that is not happening. People are channelling but they are not going any further. They access into a level and stay there, because it is safe, and they have chosen to be amazed by what they do and not use it as a tool to go further with. It has been subverted by commercialisation, and has become a product instead of a process. This is the way in which the fear energy has subverted a wonderfully important process of evolution. By distracting people from what their purpose is.

If you try to encourage people to go beyond these things, it completely frightens them. They will agree and then withdraw, because it is a concept that stretches the mind beyond its dimensions of reality. This can be frightening and seem unattainable, whereas the access of one being channelling may then seem attainable. We wish to encourage them to believe that it is possible to access this information instantaneously. All mind-sciences are attainable to every human being, but they must be pursued, exercised and used – they are tools.

The time has come, as you often say, to "walk your talk". It is time to use these tools yourself and to live with them. Spread the message to any being who begins to enquire that these are natural skills, which they may use themselves

It isn't a question of whether people are ready; it is a question of what you are going to perpetuate – followers, or leaders. There has been enough perpetuation of the sheep mentality. This is not a criticism of the concept of tribal unity, or the concept of communal assistance; but against the concept of the blind follower, the one who accepts no responsibility, who does what they are told – the mass mentality. This is no longer sufficient for the survival of your species on this planet.

There has been a subtle but efficient subversion within humankind of the move towards self-preservation and self-evolution. The forces of Fear which are the counterpart to the constant and driving desire in every being to fulfil themselves in Love, have turned an evolutionary, self enlightenment process into a commercialized product.

The watching energies (the observers) are deeply concerned that there will be so much waste before the turnabout is made, that it will put a great strain even on those who are prepared for such things. It is difficult to say what the answer is, because all of those who already know what to do, are doing it. What is important perhaps is to be very vocal, to spread the word. To get more individuals who have become used to following, to return into the realm of active participation. To get those who are withdrawing from the system, because they are discouraged by the way it functions, to recognise that they have to get back in it in order to influence it. To recognise that although you can manipulate some of the laws of physics, you also have to acknowledge that they are there, they have a purpose for being, and they must be manipulated with care and courtesy.

Whether you do it on this planet on a microscopic scale, or on a macroscopic scale, it brings you back to the universal theme of the purpose of existence, which is the re-emergence with *The One*.

The Nature of Disease and Disease Control

The emotional and mental processes, which manifest in the physical form as illness.

There is no question that a mind, which is experiencing a strong emotional trauma, will manifest that emotional trauma in the outer physical life in some way. This may be as a physical disablement, or it may be as a series of actions, happening to the individual, attracted to them by this mental output.

It is a question of the frequency at which those thoughts are taking place, and whether they are in the frequencies, which communicate outwards in the electromagnetic fields, (which deal on the same wavelengths as radio waves) or whether they are in the frequencies that go inwards to communicate with the microparticular structure of the body. You might say they are going inwards, trying to escape, and in so doing, they force the cellular structures into manifesting whatever disturbance is created.

The most obvious example of this would be a nervous stomach upset which results when someone's concern over, or anticipation of an event causes a great deal of acid to be released into that organ. Another example would be the unnecessary fear reaction known as "fight or flight" where anticipation again causes the release of adrenaline and/or other such substances to prepare the body for a crisis that does not yet exist, consequently causing diseasement.

In most cases, the thought processes cause an imbalance in the enzyme production and chemical reactions, which are part of the body's natural reactive processes. Thus, the organs, which are responsible for releasing chemical messages and substances in response to specific situations, are releasing those substances, but the situations do not exist. It is as if you were putting a medicine designed to deal with a specific disease into your body, but the disease is not there, so the medicine then becomes a poison.

In the same way, chemicals and enzymes are released by the body to deal with certain problems and situations. The thought processes have triggered these reactions, and if there is no actual problem to be dealt with, those substances then become toxic to the body. Since these substances are produced by the body, there is no antibody reaction to them. The immune system does not treat the secretions as poisonous, because they were released by the body, on command.

However, they are wandering around, with nothing to do, like a troop of military personnel, turned out to deal with a problem where there is none. Since there is no problem, they create one, because they have nothing better to do.

It is as if you have sent a platoon of soldiers to deal with a riot in a town and when they arrive there it is perfectly peaceful. They are wandering around, revved up, and ready to deal with a riot, so they proceed to cause some trouble. And that trouble can lead to the very riot they were sent to quell. They have become the source of the riot, so they cannot deal with it, and trouble brews and gets out of hand.

The body is deeply confused, not quite sure what to do. What would you do if you were a general who sent the troops in to quell a riot, and the troops themselves became the riot? You cannot send more of the same. You are not quite sure what to do. How can you correct the problem? You tell them to leave and they don't, because now they are busy creating their own riot; you are stuck! In such cases a General might have to pretend the situation does not exist. The body however, unlike a human general however, persists in looking for a solution; it is incapable of simply ignoring it.

Now, this is where the alternative therapist can assist. The alternative therapist comes in, and from the outside says "I know what to do". The therapist then clears away the confusion, and brings in the counter solution to whatever the problem is. This can be done by using light therapy, magnetic therapy, or a healing energy.

Everything calms down; the body can then carefully examine the situation and take the actions necessary. The sooner this happens in the process, the more effective it is. Like any out-of-balance condition, if unaddressed within a certain time frame, it can take on a life of its own, and go completely beyond controlling.

The world you live in reflects very accurately the processes of the human body, as you can see around you, in political situations and religious conflicts. Many situations which were minor and unimportant when they began, have escalated out of proportion, and have taken on a life of their own. Had those situations been dealt with when they began, they would never have erupted into the situations they have become.

The body causes imbalance in the same way, when what was supposed to be a stop-gap measure of protection, is turned into a conflict, which then grows and grows until it gets completely out of proportion and incorporates many things.

So, for example, in a case where there is strong self-negation, a self-hatred, for example, a feeling of diseasement with oneself, a feeling of poison inside, a message can go out, which would ultimately encourage the growth of a cancer. In this case the body is responding to a familiar message that a repair of some kind is needed. This obedient but inappropriate response of the body is to encourage cells in the emotional focus area to replicate, as they would do in a repair situation, such as in a wound. However since there is no repair needed, the replication message manifests around the emotional focus of the various disease messages sent by the mind.

A "growth" is simply the inappropriate replication of cells in an area of the body. Cancer is a situation where the cells, in the normal course of reproduction, suddenly go out of control. They begin to reproduce at a far more aggressive rate than is normal. Then, in one isolated area, certain cells begin to over-dominate. Why should this happen in a certain area? What communication might have been given? It is possible that a growth chemical has been mistakenly released; an enzyme, which facilitates reproduction for the purpose of healing in an area where there is a need for rapid reproduction.

When you wound yourself and healing is needed; a message comes down and says "focus on this area, we must reproduce most rapidly". Suppose the same message goes down to an area that is not in the need of healing? The cells respond – they know what their job is. They are supposed to reproduce accurately and very rapidly, and thus they do it, and become a disease. A message came down and said, "There is a need to repair". So what is out of balance?

When addressing this situation, you need to examine the interrelationship of the internal workings of the human body, and various thoughts and emotions. This is where the understanding of chakras[22], the various energy fields radiating from each chakra point, and an understanding of acupressure and acupuncture points (because they are along meridians, which are also related to chakra areas), becomes vital. These will show you the trouble spots that are related to general complaints.

In a variety of disorders, they can give you the specific line of connection between the thought or emotion, and the physical manifestation. You will find that every acupressure point along a given meridian, traced back to its general emotional content, will have direct connection to a specific emotional thought. A great deal of work has been done in this area[23], but there can be even more, because as you know there are hundreds of points upon the body.

The Relationship Between Thoughts Emotions and Health

Emotion is thought. Most people make the mistake of separating mental processes from feeling processes. They forget that both processes occur in the mind. Your emotion is a sensation that responds to a thought, and emotion as you know, is the tool for learning. The body goes through actions, and has experiences, which the mind and the soul embodiment, react to emotionally, so that information may be gathered.

Your mind has a thought, usually a memory or anticipation. The thought is so strong that it creates an emotional response in the soul body, either from the soul body's memory of what that thought of action should initiate, or from the memory of some observed

---

[22] *The energy centres which interface between the subtle bodies and the physical glandular system.*

[23] *Louise Hay "You Can Heal Your Life" for example.*

outside experience. Either way the experience already exists.

It is not possible for a human being to have an emotional reaction to a thought of any action they have not experienced in some way. For example, in the case of a very new, young, physical manifestation, one who has not lived many lifetimes. No matter how empathetic they may be, if they have no past life experience of a rape, or current life experience or knowledge of rape, they could not properly imagine the emotional reaction to that experience. Therefore they would never fear it. In all their imagination they could never create the diseases, which are created by a human being who is afraid of that event, or who has experienced that event. If you are living in this current lifetime and have not had any trigger from another lifetime to bring to your consciousness some of the memory of that fear, then again you will also not have that fear.

Once you have had an experience of a traumatic nature, and cleared it (that is to say, you have had the experience, you've learned the lesson, and you have expanded your compassion to incorporate the understandings learned in that experience), there is no need to repeat it in another lifetime. Therefore you will not create any of the illnesses associated with it. But at the same time, you will have a compassionate understanding of those illnesses, without having to experience the event which triggers them, and without being afraid of it happening to you.

The mental process comes first. A being has a thought or series of thoughts, which are related to past experiences. These are not necessarily past life experiences, but something they have already experienced, or something they have seen, which triggers the anticipation of the experience. These thoughts can be at the deepest level – dream level or below – they are ever-present unconscious thoughts, working at the level of the cellular structure.

These repetitive and consistent thoughts send out the message to produce whatever is necessary to counteract this event. The event however, has not taken place. It is not going to take place, and so those chemical substances and enzymes have nothing to combat. Consequently, things are getting very confused down in that area of the cellular structure. Would you not get confused, if you were doing what you know was right and suddenly there was a very strong force telling you that what you are doing is wrong? What would you do? You become paralysed. Is that not the automatic reaction? Of course it is.

For an individual there is always the probability that a moments reflection will cause a decision to be reached and an action taken.

However in the case of your cellular structure, there is no such individual, independent intelligence, Microparticular intelligence is more of a group mentality. There is not a group of individual energies each with their own mindset, discussing where they are going to go. Their way of working is to respond directly to your thought, and the stronger that thought is, the more consistent it comes out, the more likely it is to cause action.

Thus, they are going along, happily being that which they are, doing their proper work, and the message comes down that you are diseased – there is a problem and help is being sent. So they stop what they are doing, and they wait, because they do not know what to do now.

Then come the substances to cure the disease, which does not exist, and as I said, those substances wander around having nothing to do, so they begin to meddle with these other frozen little particulars, who do not know what to do.

So, in addition to a thought that has paralysed them, there is also the chemical response, which requires reaction. Imagine, you are crossing a wide road and just as you get to the mid point you see a car coming very fast! You must do something! Do you run forward, or backward? If you go the wrong way, you get hit by the car and you are dead! This is the image! Some action must be taken in response to the chemical trigger, but there is no indication as to which the correct or incorrect action may be.

This is how you get the growth of real disease. You might think of it as the little particulars stopping and saying, "What are we supposed to do?" and the chemicals coming down and saying, "Hi! I am here to cause you to grow rapidly, because there is a need for mending." And as they do not know what else to do, they immediately say, "Well that's the instruction, and you are here, so you must belong here. You could not be here if you weren't supposed to," and they begin to do it. Thus a cancer is born for example. Do you see how simple it is?

This is not to imply that all diseasement of this nature are wholly related to confused thought messages. There are many ways in which messages to the body may become confused.

The abundance of harmful chemical substances in your living environments, the massive amounts of uncontrolled radioactive particles which are manufactured and stored all over your planet, are examples of substances which can influence the bodies internal communication systems. Constant exposure to such substances creates a continuous degradation of the healthy physiological system. Your bodies cannot adjust rapidly enough to evolve defences naturally against these influences. This is why we discuss these subjects. It is time for you to take personal control of your immune systems and assist them to function more efficiently.

The best way for you to take this control is to adjust your way of thinking and by extension your life style choices. The exterior choices are already familiar to most beings since they are part of the commercial health industry. They involve the nourishment you ingest, the amount of physical activity you incorporate into your life, and the balance of rest and work activities in a daily cycle, and the nature of your surrounding environment.

The interior choices; those which concern examining your thoughts and possibly changing them deliberately, are less often addressed.

While any healers goal is to repair or remove a diseasement, even disease has a role to play in a beings life and must be examined with that understanding by both healer and client.

In the end, the overriding factor has always been that you exist to learn; to understand the nature of love and compassion to its greatest degree. All experiences in any given lifetime are part of that on-going lesson. Everything you experience serves that purpose.

Any being who accesses the information and understands that all of these experiences are for this purpose, can simplify their life greatly by understanding, learning their lessons quickly and refusing to manifest them in physical form. They don't need to manifest a lesson they have already learned. With diseasement or with any great trauma in your life, your first best internal action will be to examine the experience for what it is teaching you about the nature of expressing love and compassion. The more information you derive from the experience immediately, the more likely your chances of experiencing a healing.

This is not a certainty because it is difficult for any being to consciously draw every nuance of information in present time from any learning experience. It is inherent in the purpose of such experiences that if you already knew the lessons being learned, there would be no need of the experience. Often the learning requires a significant epiphany, which by its nature is not arrived at by delib-eration but rather as a revelation.

Understand that everything we are talking about in this publication has logic. These truths and techniques are as provable and as clear as any scientific information that you have uncovered on this planet. That is why they will prevail. Not because of some mystical belief, but because their logic and functioning are inescapable. Even by those who would contradict. It is simply the acknowledgement and the use of another science.

AIDS

In a viral life form there is no judgement. There are no questions of right or wrong. Yet there is the awareness of the right and need to survive, and in the very unusual way in which microparticular forms function, there is an awareness of artistic expression. It is creative expression; original creative thought, *Divine* thought, the needing to create and evolve, to create variations on your own form. It is an organic truth for all living intelligences, regardless of their size or simplicity.

Creative impulse; the awareness of the need for change, regardless of what seems to be the stimuli, has a strong connection with the *Divine*. All creative principles can be equated in your language with the concept of artistic expression. There is no other term that would be accurate. We cannot use the word mutation, which would most often be used in this context. Your scientific and medical communities would refer to this particular disease's ability to mutate, to evolve itself, to change its format in response to threat, as mutation.

I am offering you the thought that its ability to change is not only in response to threat. It is not simply that one sees a threat and responds immediately in a certain way. There is a processing of information that allows for a certain amount of flexible expression.

More than one choice is possible. The individual microparticular, or the communal microparticular intelligence of that life form, makes one of several choices, and those choices are not only based on the stimuli, but also on a certain link with the *Divine*. Thus is *Our* influence felt.

This viral form has become very specific in its direction, which is why it is allowed to continue. It will serve the purpose of causing human beings to re-examine their relationship to their own defensive systems, and in the process teach them to understand more deeply the nature of illness and the power of mind over illness, and to recognise that this process of change, within the physical body, is a conscious choice. HIV is an evolutionary tool. It did not come into being by accident, and is not allowed to continue by accident, nor is it simply reacting without guidance.

There is no focus on punishing any group of beings. That is simply the kind of human thought limitation that takes place when confronting events of this type. The sexual act is simply one of the most efficient methods of transferring this particular viral life form from one being to another, and certain physical relationships between human beings are more conducive to that transfer than others.

This illness has served so many functions, many of which you already know. There is, of course, the evolutionary function of changing the immune system, the literal breaking down of the current control mechanism of the immune system, which must then be rebuilt if it is to function. The HIV virus is extremely efficient in breaking down that system. Unfortunately in most cases, it moves so rapidly that the body affected does not know what is happening. Most deaths have occurred due to the victim being unaware of what they were dealing with, and the body functioning automatically in response to what was happening.

With the advent of more information and knowledge, beings who have acquired this Viral Intelligence (HIV) have found ways to prolong their existence, by delaying the body's extreme reaction to it. It is a question of being very consciously aware of how the body deals with such problems, and the awareness that there is absolutely no reason why your body cannot live in peace with this virus.

The virus is eliminating a cellular structure that, until now, has been in command of the protective functions within the body, which fight disease. All you have to do is take over that function, and then what is the problem? Even if the HIV virus chooses to consume every T cell in your body, you should, with your conscious mind, be able to take over the function of commanding the body to deal with any invaders. Thus, if you have a bacterial infection, a cold, a cut, or any of the illnesses from which human beings usually decease the body when their body does not seem to be able to combat the disease, there is no problem.[24]

You can contact the antibodies yourself, and tell your antibody production area to take action, by using the pineal, the pituitary and the other areas of the brain that have been relatively dormant, until now. You say to them, "this is the nature of this illness, I see it, I envision it, and this must be stopped." Thus creating within yourselves the necessary function to stop the particular illness.

In many cases the immune system breakdown occurs so rapidly that the human body, so conditioned to rely on the existing system, begins to succumb immediately to many other illnesses.

Thus, in disease, and in the defence of the body against disease, there is a similar transition needed. Healers of the mind, who have

---

24 *Discussed more fully in the 2nd volume under the Intelligent Immune System*

dealt with the subject of healing by the power of thought, or have utilised different healing energies, such as hands-on energy healing, sound healing, light healing, etc., have incorporated this awareness in themselves. By communicating this in their books and other forms of communication, they have begun to excite humanity into initiating the appropriate changes in the physical body. Eventually the body will deal with foreign substances in a different manner, no longer reliant on the system that was incorporated into the physical body for automatic physical reaction.

This is a process that begins to awaken the human mind to scanning its own body. You (Elizabeth) are well aware of your own ability to know when something is wrong, to know why it is wrong and where it comes from. If it seems to be something that you yourself cannot handle, you know whom to go to for assistance in the analysis and probable treatment. This has been a gift that you have been aware of for a long time, but in many beings this gift was suppressed a long time ago, and they have become quite dependant on the autonomic physical functions of their body without conscious thought.

Like so many other things related to the exercise of the human mind, and the reawakening of many skills, mastering these skills requires a pattern of discipline, calling for a combination of meditative and higher vibrational thought. However, some beings cannot utilise the conventional meditative forms – which is not a prevention to the acquiring of information and understanding about the nature of the body. Techniques and information may be acquired, either through the physical input means of reading and other outside information, or by turning within and accessing those vibrations of communication within the body.

The thought that so many human beings must die, is perhaps the most difficult thing for a compassionate human being to deal with at this time. The evolution of humankind unfortunately does not eliminate the concept of death, and not every human being born on the planet at this time is at the same evolutionary level. There is nothing new about this, and it must not be taken personally. This is not a call to say, "Ah, those of you who are clever enough to read this material are therefore superior and far ahead of your brothers and sisters." It is true that you have put yourself in a position where you can acquire this information, but you who read it may be just as careless about utilising it as one who never had access to it.

There are those who will never have access to it, who will have access to other sources of information that will be attracted to them, because of the purity of their nature or their relationship to other healing forms that essentially exercise the same function regardless of the language. There are people whose relationship to the function of land and nature is so acute and organic, that their response to any disturbance of the body as severe as that of HIV would be to go back to the simplicity of their roots. And in that act, combining both the faith and knowledge of the energy and nature of the planet to preserve them, would defeat the illness without even realising what they had done.

Of course, it is often true that those who feel they have access to unusual information decide immediately that they are the only ones who will survive. This has nothing to do with it. This information, offered in this manner, is here for those people who will acquire it in this way.

AIDS is not a punishment upon those who contract it.

It is part of the transition and pattern of their lives, and there are those who must succumb to this illness and die, in order to cause more focus to be put on those who survive. Some have elected to succumb to the illness so that information can be gathered from their experiences. It simply seems more tragic, because many of the beings who have succumbed have contributed great things to the culture of your world. For a long time many ignorant beings have thought, that these deaths had something to do with the expression of physical love, which as I said, is only a physical means of transmission.

Another function of AIDS is the elimination of population. It provides a means for significant decrease in the population in places where other means of reduction would not be efficient. In places where there is not a great deal of war or other forms of elimination, disease is the function that often comes into play. This results in the remaining population activating the many alternative ways in which to utilise defensive systems within the body. This works in tandem with the evolution of physical humankind.

There is an interesting side effect – again it was not really part of the plan, but is one of those wonderful creative variations that we would like to encourage – which is the re-examination of the nature of relationships. The need of beings to recognise that it is helpful to know the whole being before you share a loving expression, regardless of whether it is a mental, emotional or physical expression. There is greater joy in it, and it is a more evolved way to be. This is not to place a limitation on physical expression but simply the recognition that it is a human being you are loving. That there is a physical and emotional connection between two beings, not simply a series of pegs and holes. This unfortunately seems to be the mentalities of so many, especially those who have chosen an alternative physical expression.

In so many cases, their judgement of themselves, has limited the joys that they can gain from that expression. They rarely find themselves looking for what they would have looked for, if they had chosen a more conventional expression of relationship. Unfortunately, that is part of the system passed down to them. It is the most insidious, prejudiced programming that has ever been laid upon those (especially the male of your species), who chose to express their physical love to another of their own sex. It is the most horrendous oppression; so subtle is it, that they perpetuate their own repression.

What is needed is not simply an act of acceptance, it is awareness that they are also entitled to come to know each other slowly, to become friends, to fall in love, and then to want to share that loving expression. Liaisons performed in alleyways and other such places, were never what a loving expression was about. This by itself is a condemnation that perpetuates the self-negation, "I am nothing but an object, the person I am with is nothing but an object, and we are simply relieving an urge." How animalistic, how primitive, regardless of whether it is two beings of one sex or two beings of opposite sexes – it is irrelevant. If that is what you wish then it doesn't matter who you are dealing with and you might as well use an animal or a plastic figure.

So, the advent of this illness, through its fear of contagion, has begun to awaken many of these individuals. Not all unfortunately, some simply cannot take the awareness of relationships and have become quite fatalistic. They will perpetuate this illness and will most probably die or cause the death of many others. It is not something to handle lightly. I may give you much information on how it may be dealt with, yet this does not mean that everyone will do it or be able to do it, or even choose to do it or believe it can be done.

It is also an exercise in the humbling of the conventional scientific and medical communities, to open up their minds (a very difficult task I might add) to the fact that "There are more things in Heaven and Earth Horatio, than are dreamt of in your philosophy.[25] " A very nicely turned phrase, I think. However it is also a great truth.

AIDS is attracted and supported by self-negation, by those thoughts of feeling unworthy, unwell, wrong, incorrect, etc. Any such thought will support a disease of any kind whose function is to consume some part of the body. Those thoughts support the viral intelligence's notion that it is performing a useful function, because it is obviously removing something that is of no use, or is unworthy.

As you know, viral intelligence functions on a general command basis, and if these intelligent particles are picking up support for destruction, they are encouraged to grow even more rapidly. Another example is when, even though one is not feeling hostile towards themselves, there is great fear of what is occurring. The fear usually generates a series of chemicals that excite the viral process. This is similar to being afraid of an animal – it will be drawn to you, due to a chemical response that is given off.

Microparticular intelligence is no different, they do not mean to be hostile but they are drawn. So the fear of the illness, and that terrible tendency to feel unworthy of survival, will encourage this illness.

Defiance that comes from fear, does not serve as efficiently in the conquering of this illness, as defiance with joy. The part of the body that says "I will not succumb to this; I can beat it if I do these

---

25 *Shakespeare: Hamlet — Act I, Scene V.*

things," is better than when the operative force is "I will die if I do not beat it." The latter will delay the process but will not overcome it. The affirmation "I simply do not choose to acknowledge that this has power," backed up with actions to support the body – the changing of diet, the initiation of exercise, etc., will be interpreted by the microparticular intelligences as support and love. It is not just a question of the doing of it. It is the fact that the action of the doing is the action of saying "I love this form. I will support this form. I am taking the actions necessary to communicate that."

The physicalisation of the idea is very important, because through the physicalisation of the thought – **first there was the thought and then the word, and then the action is the completion of the process of a thought coming into being** – it then becomes reality. This is information that is useful in any context.

For any being, there is always first the thought, then there is the voicing of the thought, but then the thought and the voicing must be put into action. When action is taken, regardless of the significance of the action, it is symbolic of the bringing-into-being of the thought. Once action is taken the body's microparticular intelligences will respond very effectively to it. So those beings who are aware of this will initiate an action, such as the changing of the physical form. It may only require the intention, and the actual performing of the act for only one day, it is symbolic. Even if it is done once a week or for a short time, there will still be a physical reaction.

Scientists have been doing their research in the wrong direction. They have rejected many creative solutions, and having exhausted all the conventional options over the last 10 or 15 years, they are now reaching out to the communities, which have been dealing with these problems. They are beginning to notice anomalies that they haven't seen before. For example, that high risk groups in many cases though not immune, have the illness, but do not seem to be succumbing to it. How is this possible and what does this mean to humanity in general?

So a great deal of new valuable information for your community will come out of these researches. Not perhaps what is expected, but many other things, not the least important of which, is the awareness that as humankind continues to destroy its natural environment, many solutions to the illnesses that exist are also being destroyed. This planet was created to provide an answer to every problem. There is no illness on this planet that cannot be cured by something native to it. But humankind has laboured long and hard to destroy many areas, in order to give itself what it thinks it needs.

Consequently, there are diseases coming into being for which the answers provided are no longer there, or are in such small quantities that they cannot be found. Thus humanity is forced to turn inwards and utilise the powers of material control, manifestation, matter creation, and manipulation, to deal with these things perhaps a little bit sooner than it might have had to. This is far more difficult than taking an herbal concoction. You have created your own most difficult task. Humanity busily shovels large mountains and barriers in its own path, to climb over, as they theoretically create what they want and then wonder why it is so difficult to achieve. That is your way of learning.

Other diseases
There is a desperate need for balance of the number of life-forms on this planet, and it is almost impossible to maintain that balance because of the level of reproduction and the mistaken need to prolong life beyond its actual function. Thus, as your scientists

begin to explore ways to control certain illnesses, there will always be others coming into being or familiar ones that are revived.

In the next few years, the illness known on your planet as Tuberculosis (TB) will also experience an evolution. It is also an intelligent form, not quite as forceful as HIV, which is evolving and will continue to evolve and will always evolve; there is no way to stop that. The only control for it is to basically say, "That's all right you're safe, you do not have to evolve, you're fine the way you are."

The trick with HIV and TB is to cause it not to want to disturb itself. To basically say, "Relax, you are in a nice safe home, you do not have to change. You do not have to consume anything, just go to sleep," and being a nice lazy intelligence it will do that. It only wants to feel safe.

Tuberculosis will undergo a series of transformations making it once again more difficult to control than the original form. The biggest mistake the medical community will make will be to try to control it in the way it was controlled before; not recognising that this is a mutated form. Therefore the various controls and cures will not serve to eliminate this illness.

Again such illnesses are best conquered by the maintenance of a viable healthy physical form. To maintain the body in health and vigour, it should be kept as free of toxins as possible, by not taking into the body unnecessary toxins. The cleaner you are, the stronger your body is. It is a matter of loving the self and maintaining its everyday vibration at the highest frequency you are comfortable with. This automatically makes it more difficult for illness to occur, so disease finds no purchase in the form. It is automatically uncomfortable and therefore, will not choose to stay. Disease only has power when there is weakness or resignation to it.

For those very good, very dedicated and pure people, who still find themselves succumbing to these illnesses, there is no punishment intended. It is not a bad thing, nor have they failed to do their best. It is simply that this is their time and this was the way chosen.

This is probably the information most people exploring these philosophies have the hardest time understanding. It is one thing to accept it as a thought, and another to live with it as a reality. It is a very uncomfortable thought as well, for the being living it; there is always the question, "Why is this happening to me? If I can do so many things, why am I not controlling this?"

There are always aspects of your physical form that need to express themselves. Toxic release may or may not manifest a diseasement. You (Elizabeth) have already experienced what would be, for someone else a severe and life-threatening situation, but for you it was simply a problem that has to be focused on[26].

Such problems cannot be ignored, they must be dealt with, and once you have started to deal with your problems you get them under more control and eventually conquer them completely.

---

26 *A heart problem that was corrected by the use of mind techniques – E*

The Participation Of The Individual In Universal Process

The most important thought for any individual to remember, is that their every action, plays a part in the overall scheme of things. The saddest effect of the existing social influences is that an individual is considered to be unimportant unless they have achieved a position of external power or wealth.

The simple act of *example* has been neglected in the thought process.

It takes so little effort to do a thing that others may see, agree with and eventually copy. You need to recognize that all essential teaching is an act of expression and imitation.

When a child first begins to learn something they don't know what it is they are learning. They simply imitate and eventually the actions take on meaning. So it is with all beings in form. The reason it is important for beings who are conscious to live their truth, is so that others may see them doing it, and copy that behaviour.

The advantage to the pervasion of information, which has taken place in what you call this New Age, is that by imitation there will be a considerable number who will learn something – even if they don't understand what they are doing in the meantime. It is due to this lack of understanding, that many drop-out, or remain stuck in the pattern of seeking. They become the ever-seeking, because they are not very sure what it is they are looking for – and if they did find it, it would frighten them anyway. It doesn't matter though. In the pattern of repeating and imitating what you have seen, something is learned even if it is not understood.

For those of you who are used to understanding something after experiencing it once, or who get frustrated continually with those who do not see the obvious, it is a lesson in humility and understanding of the process. It should be understood that all beings are not equipped to comprehend to the same degree at the same time, any more than a 3-year-old can comprehend with the depth of a 10-year-old. The same sequence of events takes on a different meaning as you grow with maturity and understanding, and bring to a given experience a wider range of related experiences. So it is important to be allowing of those who imitate poorly, what they see you do. They try, but the imitation is simply not terribly convincing. It is unsuccessful because they are imitating the surface of what they see instead of the deeper meaning.

So each individual performs their own act of creative participation in the whole. The most important thing is that they come to realise it, accept it, own it, and take it as their responsibility.

Is it not true that if you pick up your own refuse, you may inspire another to do the same; that if you take the time to stop an argument in the street, another person may get the idea that they can do that as well? You take your own action. You simply be it, and through another's act of imitation you have created a movement. Then the movement becomes a wave and a pattern, and the pattern then merges itself into a reality, a new existence.

Even successful mutation is nothing more than imitation, although it is occurring on a multi-cellular level. Mutation is not really accidental. What a concept!

Isn't it interesting how human beings, when faced with a scientific concept that they do not understand, acknowledge randomness, chaos, or accident as a viable scientific truth, instead of recognising a creative response?

Mutation is a choice, made at a micro-cellular level in agreement with universal truth; the coming into being of a change in form, is registered by the microparticles, the cellular structure of other related beings, who choose then to imitate it. Natural selection is an act of imitation.

It's really extremely simple. The simplicity of truth is the thing most distressing, in most cases, to the scientific mind. They long for it to be as convoluted as the systems they have devised for discovering the truth. But the truth that they are discovering is essentially simple. It is the systems that are convoluted and confusing. Just as when a thought that is being expressed is essentially simple, but the language can be more or less complicated as the case may be.

So, it is important to stress to all who would access this information that their individual participation is vital, absolutely vital! There is no such thing as, 'it doesn't matter'.

This is important!

It does matter. It matters in every moment. There must be constant awareness that any action that you take, or choose not to take, will have an effect on something. You must also recognise that acknowledgment for such an act may not be forthcoming outside of you. Therefore, it is important that you, yourself, recognise the significance of the actions you are taking.

This is very difficult even for those who are more enlightened, as there is always a need to have some acknowledgment of what they are doing. If you spend time worrying about whether or not your actions are being noticed, you stay with the actions that get noticed, instead of letting them go and continuing forward – into the unknown.

Go forward – secure in the knowing that your every act, thought and feeling is acknowledged and respected by those who watch and love you very much

The Story

This is *The Story* of why existence came into being. It is a story, which in its every instance is symbolic. It is a story, which should be shared from one living physical Teacher, to another living physical Being or Searcher. For our purpose, it is important that those who read this book at least have the option of accessing the information.

In the beginning there was That Which Is.

That Which Is, a thought of love in totality – without conditions, without limitations, with compassion. That Which Is – GOD.

And That Which Is God, for the Joy of the re experiencing of Itself, caused to come into being the first separation. The first existence. The first illusion.

And there came into being that which we may call A God – all knowing, all powerful, all everything.

A God – A Thought of Love in totality, without conditions, without limitations, except for the awareness of Itself as separate.

A God was in joy to be A God – and had a wonderful time being A God doing everything that anyone could imagine A God should, or would do. Creating universes, planets, life forms, and manifesting in all forms of existence other than the frequency of itself.

But, A God became aware that something was missing.

It was all knowing. It was all powerful. It was all everything, and yet... something was missing. No matter what it did, or how it expressed itself, it could not find out what was missing.

And so – A God came to understand it was too great, too powerful, to find out what was missing.

In order to find out what was missing, A God chose to forget that which it was – chose to take on a limitation, and create the second illusion. A God forgot it was A God, and caused to come into being that which we may call A God as Light.

And A God as Light was all powerful and all knowing, and indeed without limitation, except for now being in the awareness of Itself as Light.

A God as Light had a wonderful time manifesting in all forms of existence other than the frequency of itself.

But A God as Light, being Itself, became aware that something was missing. But it was too powerful to understand what was missing.

Therefore, in order to find out what was missing, A God as Light, chose to take on another limitation, and create an illusion – forget some part of itself.

A God as Light coalesced into form and there came into being, Light in Form.

Light in Form was still very powerful indeed – no longer A God, but a form of light. Light in Form...

Even though Light in Form had to travel in Form throughout whatever universes it was in, it still had a wonderful time being

Light in Form. It enjoyed the being of itself.

In all of its manifestations and awarenesses it came to understand that there was a discontent. There was something that was missing... Light in Form wanted to discover what was missing.

So Light in Form, in order to discover what was missing, chose to forget some part of what it was – to take on a limitation, and cloud itself in another illusion. So there came into being the coalescence of light form into embodiment. And there came into being a Light Body – a physical body of light – not simply form, but an embodiment of light.

Light Body was indeed a limitation, for now light must travel within the limitations of the embodiment.

It did so and was able to manifest many forms of existence below the frequency of itself as it searched and searched.

But it did not know what it was searching for. There came the time when the Light embodiment knew that there was an emptiness, somewhere inside.

There was something missing.

The Light Embodiment, in order to find out what was missing, chose to forget some part of itself – chose to take on a limitation and created an illusion. In order to find out what was missing it caused to come into being the Ego. The awareness of the Self.

There came into being the Light Being. Now light not only existed as an embodiment, but also had a Being, an identity – that which you may call, the Ego.

The Light Being, in its own awareness was very powerful. For you see, in each manifestation there is a complete forgetting of the manifestation prior. Therefore, no being, once it takes on this illusion, has the memory of what it was before.

The Light Being existed in the totality of itself and was able to understand that there was a mission. For it is only the Being who can understand the nature of mission.

The Light Being travelled hither and yon throughout the Universe of its existence, manifesting into many forms, having many experiences, but a feeling of vague disquiet remained. It could not find out what its mission was. It had a mission – but what was this mission? There was simply the awareness of something unfulfilled. Something was missing.
Something is always missing!
The Light Being came to understand that in order to find out what was missing it would have to create that which could identify and retain the concept of a mission.

So the Light Being in order to find out what was missing, and fulfil its mission, chose to forget some part of itself – to take on a limitation, and create an illusion.

So there came into being the Essential Spirit of Unified Polarity.

Now the Essential Spirit, which overlays the Light Being, has face, and figure and form that is consistent. Indeed, a personality manifestation, which is a refinement of the personality, which existed in the Light Being (the Ego).

The Essential Spirit of Unified Polarity knew its mission. It knew it must find out what was missing, and that its purpose was to experience and retain information, in order to find out what was missing.

So the Essential Spirit manifested into all forms of existence lower than the frequency of itself – in unified polarity. It retained a great deal of information, but there was an essential understanding that was missing from the retention of the information. This caused it to never completely understand the nature of its mission – to find out what was missing.

For how can something be missing from a unified polarity? It is unified by its definition!

Thus the Essential Spirit of Unified Polarity recognised that in order to find out what was missing, to properly assemble the information necessary, it would have to create the understanding of "missing" – of absence, of incompletion.

Therefore the Unified Spirit took the most dramatic and courageous action in the entire line of existence, for this action, once taken, could not be undone. The Unified Essential Spirit chose to forget that it was a unified polarity field, and separated itself for all time into two essential spirits.

There came into being Male and Female Essential Spirits, positive and negative energy, opposing polarities, electric/magnetic, two fields – each of them from that time forward having their own mission, their own direction, their own something which was missing, which has to be fulfilled.

Your Essential Spirit is here, and lives at this frequency of vibration.

You are that which is a light being clothed in an essential spirit. You have a personality, a face, a figure, a form, an identity, and a mission.

Your mission is to find out what is missing.

The purpose of the Essential Spirit is to assemble, gather and collate the information gained through life experience, in order to find out what is missing.

The Essential Spirit does not feel, it has no judgement on any action, emotion or piece of knowledge. It has only this one purpose.

The Essential Spirit, because it cannot feel, can only assemble information, and so it is the perfect tool for pursuing a focused mission.

Each essential spirit, when the choice is made to manifest in physical form, creates the Soul Embodiment.

The Soul Embodiment is the astral image of the physical body it is going to inhabit. This is true whether the form is human, or alien (another species on another planet). It is also true for animal life on a separate frequency line.

There is an embodiment created, which we are calling soul – the non physical representation of the physical form it is going to be in.

The Soul Embodiment is created for the purpose of holding and utilising emotion – which is the tool through which you learn.

The Soul Embodiment, at the appropriate moment, enters into the physical body, and the body is born upon the planet.

The physical body, whatever it's form, goes through active experiences, to which the Soul Embodiment reacts emotionally, and learning takes place. Information is gathered and knowledge exists.

When the physical body is deceased, the Soul Embodiment ascends the physical body, moving at increasingly higher frequencies of vibration, towards what is perceived as a light.

When it achieves a certain frequency of vibration, the Soul Embodiment dissipates, and what is left is the Essential Spirit with it's storehouse of knowledge. The information gained during that lifetime.

This information is examined and collated and a choice is made as to what form of incarnation will best serve to continue the completion of the mission.

This is all done for the purpose of finding out what is missing.

The Essential Spirit can remember and understand many things.

Your essential spirit through the experience of lifetimes and the assembling of knowledge, can remember while remaining itself, what it was to be a singular polarity.

It may remain itself and still come to the complete understanding and integration of the information that it is not a separate polarity, but a single polarity. It can remember that and continue to exist.

Your essential spirit through the experience of lifetimes and the assembling of knowledge, can remember that it is not an essential spirit at all, that it is in actuality a Light Being, without the limitations of figure and form. It can remember that, and continue to be an essential spirit, living with that understanding and therefore a higher frequency of vibration. It can remember that and continue to exist.

Your essential spirit through the experience of lifetimes and the assembling of knowledge, can remember when it was a Light Embodiment, without even the understanding of Being, without even an Ego.

Your essential spirit while maintaining the awareness of itself, can remember that it is nothing other than a light embodiment. It can remember that, and that memory can exist and be manifested by you, in your physical body, on the planet.

All evolving states of awareness, achieved by your essential spirit can be manifested in your physical form on the planet. It can be done, and it is done.

Your essential spirit, through the information gathered in lifetimes, can remember when it was merely Light in Form, and not even an embodiment. Your essential spirit, can remember what it is to be Light in Form, and continue to exist, in and of itself.

You may manifest that understanding of your essential spirit in your body on a planet. You may do this and continue to exist. You can exist with this scope of understanding in a body.

Your essential spirit, through the experience of lifetimes, may remember when it was A God as Light. You may do this and continue to exist. You exist with this scope of understanding.

A God as Light, not even form.

Your essential spirit may exist with the understanding of what it is to be A God as Light and you may manifest that understanding in your physical body on a planet.

Your essential spirit through the experience of lifetimes may come to understand the scope of what it is to be A God, a thought of Love in Totality, without conditions, or limitations, except for the awareness of itself as A God, without even the limitation of light.

Your essential spirit may come to know that, and you may manifest that knowing in a body on the planet. It is possible. It has been done and is done. Your essential spirit may know this and continue to exist.

But that is where the capacity of Essential Spirit ceases. For A God, in all the glory and awareness of Itself, could not find out what was missing.

That is where the search stops. Where it began.

There is only one place from which the Essential Spirit can find out what is missing.

There is only one place from which A God can find out what is missing........

From physical form... from the place of lowest frequency density.

From here, in an instant, an essential spirit, having achieved the awareness of what it is to be A God, and manifesting in physical form, may achieve the intuitive leap of understanding, which allows for total re emergence into That Which Is – A Thought of Love in Totality, without conditions, without limitations, WITH COMPASSION.

For what was missing from A God – in the awareness of itself as separate – was the absence in the concept of unconditional love – of Compassion.

The understanding of Compassion is that which can only be learned in the manifestation of a physical form.

The Essential Spirit is that which can comprehend in totality the understanding of love without conditions or limitations.

Compassion is learned and understood only in the physical form. Thus, for those who make the choice, there will come a moment so fulfilling of love, so complete, so total, so all encompassing, so overwhelming, that nothing other than that will do.

In that instant, the Being is so full of Love and Compassion for all existence, and even that which does not exist, that it can no longer endure separation of any kind.

It is an act of love so overwhelming, so fulfilling, so complete, so all encompassing, that it cannot be contained by any limitation of form – not even the limitation of separateness, the limitation of being - A God.

That Which is Love without conditions, with compassion, that which cannot be contained, is That Which Is - God.

That is exactly who you are.

And all you have to do is Remember!

Appendix A

The following is an alternatative version of The Story. We were concerned that the information was a repetition of other sections of the book; but at the same time felt the information was important. So we decided to give you the choice to read it if you wished without inhibiting the flow of the book

All matters which are shared with you in this book relate to all those essences of embodiment which begin with the essential spirit of unified polarity as its highest expression of frequency energy existence. The unified polarity of essential spirit – which has a face, an identity, a figure, a form, a personality if you will, but no separation between the polarities; there is no female or male definition in that essential spirit – does ultimately divide itself into two essential spirits. They are identical in every way with the exception of there being opposing polarities.

Whenever we speak of a polarity, negative and positive, or electric a magnetic, we are referring to the analogies consistent with male and female. The purpose of the Essential Spirit is to assemble all information gained in any lifetime. This information is collated and understood, and it is the essential spirit, in its individual polarities, which will decide what nature of lifetime will subsequently exist in order to further its growth and understanding of That Which It Is. Guides, teachers and other influences on these decisions usually exist at the level of unified essential spirit or high frequencies of vibration as recently enumerated.

A teacher of this type, who has been in Physical Body and has ascended that body, may choose to ascend to any one of the levels of higher frequency which have been expressed, and they will remain there until such time as they choose to re-manifest in a physical form for the completion of their journey.

Once decisions regarding the lifetime have been made the essential spirit of specific polarity will create for itself a soul embodiment. The soul embodiment is the astral image of the Physical Body it is going to inhabit. The Physical Body will express itself as a physical image of the image created by the essential spirit.

The soul embodiment is the source and wellspring of all emotional reaction. It will incorporate within it those aspects of the being which may be associated with cellular memory, with past life experiences and those many things that may affect an individual in its current lifetime body. The Physical Body, when born upon the planet, makes a choice of continued existence; once a choice has been firmly made the soul embodiment, which is in alignment with it, becomes bound to it.

The tether which binds the soul embodiment to the Physical Body is locked into the Physical Body once the Physical Body makes the choice to continue in existence. The soul embodiment receives the exact dimensions of the physical embodiment once it has entered the physical embodiment and it will continue to do so throughout the physical existence of that body. With the locking into of the Physical Body the soul embodiment forgets itself; and this is vital for if it did not it would not choose to remain in the Physical Body and death would occur. The only exception to this is if, for any reason, the physical manifestation is required to experience premature birth or any other similar or related experience. If there is some need in the Essential Spirit for the memory of that experience, then there shall be the unusual step of the soul embodiment inhabiting and locking itself into the Physical Body before it has made that physical expression into itself on the planet; but that is a rare occurrence.

Further explanation of the specifics of the relationship between the soul embodiment and the Physical Body cannot serve you at this time, but there are many complexities and they will be discussed in another volume.

The Physical Body is born upon the planet; the soul embodiment locks its essence into the Physical Body, they then align themselves and continue their physical existence. In all experiences the physical embodiment is designed to have, the soul embodiment will react with an emotional response which will generate information and learning. All learning is related to one essential purpose; the understanding of the nature of love without conditions and compassion.

The Soul Embodiment and Physical Embodiment are separate energies until the being, who has gone through the necessary sequence of significant lifetimes and made the choice to complete. This is rare; it has not been done frequently and the process is separate from enlightenment in general, as with an Avatar, Buddha or beings that are designed in their specificity to be teachers. For they must maintain some essence of existence in order to continue to teach in the way it is understood by your species.

The Journey Back

When a being is dying the entire progress of existence is reversed to the level of the essential spirit of specific polarity. A Physical Body ceases to exist, the astral body – soul embodiment, which exists in a higher frequency of existence, with its storehouse of information and experiences, ascends the Physical Body. The tether to the body is severed and it is now free. It continues to ascend; constantly increasing in frequency until its image dissipates, and what is left is the essential spirit of specific polarity, not with the emotions experienced, but with the knowledge and information gained concerning love and compassion.

At this point the essential spirit will, in conference with its wise teachers, choose the next lifetime and the experiences to be undergone for the purpose of learning the next series of lessons. And this will continue on until such time as the essential spirit has remembered in totality, all of the levels of existence, including those at higher frequencies than its own.

It is only at that point that a final lifetime may be manifested, and the ultimate understanding of love and compassion may be achieved; at that moment there is the total dissipation of all understanding of limited existence and the remembering only of That Which Is.

It is an important choice for any being to decide whether or not such an experience is appropriate for them in any given lifetime. Once the choice is made and the experience is undergone there is a definite and understandable change in the beings focus of its existence from that time forward. How the change manifests varies in many different beings, but the change when it occurs is permanent for that lifetime. You cannot essentially un-know what you know or remember in the course of the relating of this story.

Elizabeth Campbell

This book is the culmination of a very long journey for me, and has been a work of love and personal process spanning much of my life. The motivation to write this book came in response to our need to understand the seemingly complex issues of the time, to clarify misunderstandings, and learn more about the process of existence.

I started communicating with the energy that I define as Herméas in 1983. The story of how that came about would fill a volume on its own, and therefore will have to wait for another time. The channelling sessions contained in this book were received between August 1993 and December 1994, and were recorded on tape to be later transcribed and edited.

My relationship to Herméas is one of loving respect, which so deeply penetrates my being that it is very hard to define in words. Over the years we have developed a bantering style much suited to my sense of humour and stubbornness, and in some places this has spilled over into the book. So please, be aware, that if an element of this comes through the dialogue it is an aspect of our relationship and the personality definition that I have created to facilitate this communication.

The limitation of verbal communication has been one of the most challenging aspects of this project. Translating images and concepts into words was more difficult than Martha and I ever imagined. The original transcripts were wordy and cumbersome when transferred to the written word, and yet it has been difficult to cut it back without limiting the expression. We have tried to maintain a middle ground, between ease of reading and simplifying it to the point of vagueness.

Writing this book has been a catalytic event in both our lives, with major processing taking place along the way. As with any work of this kind, there has to be an owning of the material, and the outworking of that has certainly been interesting. I would like to take this opportunity to thank the many steadfast souls who have supported me in getting to this point. Without the help of the backup crew we would never get anywhere, I'm sure. I am grateful to my parents for the DNA, and allowing me to be 'sensitive', my children and family, the mystic travellers who over the years have materialised in my life, pressed buttons and moved on, and all those wonderful cosmic elves who are there for me everyday – you know who you are!

Elizabeth.

Martha E Randolph

This was Elizabeth's idea. Even though I have been able to channel for a long time, it never occurred to me that I would use that tool in the creating of a book.

I'd had a very traumatic experience during my last of three visits to Spain, where I had been teaching Spiritual Philosophy. I returned to Perth, emotionally, spiritually, and mentally exhausted, and depressed, and had lost all faith in my spiritual growth. I was deep in the "Dark Night of the Soul". Out of concern for my well-being, and in order to "get me back up on the horse", Elizabeth invited me to her house and asked me to get in touch with her friend Hermes . All I would have to do was relax, and let her bring up the frequency in the room to the point where he could talk to me, and I would then pass it on to her.

As we accelerated the energy, I began to feel alignment taking place, since direct channelling (the frequency communicated directly to my brain, and the words come out of my mouth in the is easy and comfortable for me. I began to fight it, because I was still hurt and angry at myself and all my spiritual growth, which I was busy doubting from my deepest fears.

Well, I said something about the struggle, and Elizabeth began to emit the most intricate and musical series of burps and belches that I had ever heard. They just kept on and on, and I was reduced to a pathetic blob of helpless hysterical laughter. In the midst of this, alignment took place and Herméas (his preferred pronouncement of his name) began to speak. I was fully aware of what had happened and what was being said, and I was in agreement with it. I knew that my reluctance was an expression of my fears, not my love.

Elizabeth and I began to meet regularly to share this channelling, just for the joy of it. But sometimes the information was so exciting and clarifying, and our ability to remember what was said so inconsistent, that we decided to tape the sessions. Elizabeth knew it was a book before I did.

In the process of channelling this information, and during my close association with Elizabeth, I have been forced to see many things about myself that I was completely unaware of before.

The channelling of Herméas, and the working on the printed words in this book have been a most vital part of my continuing spiritual growth, and was the only Light that could lead me out of the Dark Night of the Soul.

I don't seem to be all the way out of that feeling, but I thank That Which Is…, for manifesting as Herméas and Elizabeth Campbell, at this time in my life.

I acknowledge my most important teachers of spiritual thought in this lifetime. Katheryn Hayward, a little, bright eyed, feisty old lady whose first words to me were: "You are here to find out who you are. You are God. That is all I really have to tell you". MAFU, an out-of-body teacher who is still teaching through the body of the former Penny Torres. MAFU first told me "The Story", and it changed my life forever.

And, the master Healer and all round good guy, Dennis Adams, who made that story a viable part of my present lifetime and showed me what it means to be committed to a Spiritual Truth.

I thank you and love you all.

Martha

REGISTER FOR FREE AT www.hermeas.org for additional information, insights and teachings by Hermeas.

Registered members have exclusive access to excerpts from upcoming books, podcasts of channeled secessions with Herméas and timely messages and teachings on current events.

Martha and Elizabeth are experienced lecturers on a range of philosophical and spiritual subjects and are available for

The Intelligent Immune System

We have included some sections from the second book to give you a taste of what's to come!

We chose this chapter as one of the most important for the times to come. This information has been summarised due to limited space. We have done this as the information is complex and challenging at times and taken as a straight lift might misinform rather inform.

The immune system functions through the communication via organs that send out communicative chemicals, telling the other organs what to do to produce cells to perform particular functions. With the normal evolution of the system this process adapts over time, it is the genetic adjustment. The human immune system is currently designed to function in this manner; however this design is in the process of evolutionary revision.

In the normal course of events, in cases of serious illness, a strong individual will survive to reproduce whereas other individuals with weaker immune systems do not, and therefore you have the constant upgrading of the human system by genetic adjustment. The problem is that through medical intervention, you prolong life and assist in the reproduction of human life of those who would not have otherwise reproduced.

This unfortunately perpetuates the human race in a limited physical form, because if an individual is not able to reproduce, assisting them to reproduce simply creates a child it is going to pass on the genetic structures of one who cannot reproduce. If you have an individual who was born with the genetic programming to have a defective heart, and you allow it to live and reproduce by giving it a brand-new heart through transplant surgery, then you are perpetuating the genetic structure that is inclined to go to defective heart.

Now this does not sound very compassionate. It is however, the way the structure of evolution was designed. The divine requires that the physical embodiment evolves together with its mental, emotional and spiritual evolvement. However, because of the intervention of medical science, the next levels of evolution will have to be by conscious choice. This is why you need to begin to explore the ability of mind over microparticular structure, because mutation has been almost effectively eliminated by the practice of medicine. So you must begin to take charge of mutation, because the disease forms are evolving to a level beyond the ability of your compromised immune development to cope.

Medication may prolong the lives of human beings, but by doing so it eliminates any other process outside of its own interference within the system. This means that the processes by which certain illnesses are cured, also eliminates the possibility of a healthier stronger immune system being able to defeat the illness and survive, this allows the illness to continue, leading to eventual loss of population where such intervention is unavailable. More beings live longer due to medical influence, but they also become dependant on that influence for their continued health and life...

⌇

Ultimately the interrelatedness of all things is dependent upon the understanding of the nature of existence. Existence is infinitely flexible, and the salvaged premature child, or the person with a replaced damaged heart, will always have a role to play in the evolution of the species, but not in the development of the immune system...

⌇

The accelerated and intelligent immune system is required to fight and conquer diseases that influence the normal cellular functions of the body. It is intended to affect foreign organic forms that have evolved naturally over time and in response to human influences.

⌇

In order to create a more intelligent immune system now that mutation is effectively eliminated, you must begin to practice by utilizing your conscious mind to encourage the body to develop in that way. If the ability to develop an automatic intelligent immune system naturally has been almost eliminated then you have to develop an immune system which will respond to your conscious and deliberate direction and thought. The intelligent immune system is a more consciously directable and responsive system which adjusts itself according to the information you supply it with. It is time to educate the system.

> *The complete chapter explains in depth what the Intelligent Immune System is and why it is necessary, discusses some of the philosophical and ethical issues related to it. As with other chapters in the second book Herméas gives advice and techniques on how to develop and utilise these new tools of Mind Science.*

> *For more information go to our website www.hermeas.org*

www.ingramcontent.com/pod-product-compliance
Lightning Source LLC
La Vergne TN
LVHW011240080426
835509LV00005B/567